STUDENT GUIDANCE AND DEVELOPMENT

Mary Ann Ward
Dode Worsham

EYE ON EDUCATION
6 Depot Way West, Suite 106
Larchmont, N.Y. 10538

Copyright © 1998 Eye On Education, Inc.
All Rights Reserved.

For information about permission to reproduce selections from this book, write: Eye On Education, Permissions Dept., 6 Depot Way West, Suite 106, Larchmont, N.Y. 10538.

ISBN 1-883001-47-1

Library of Congress Cataloging-in-Publication Data

```
Ward, Mary Ann, 1946-
    Student guidance and development / Mary Ann Ward, Dode Worsham.
      p.   cm. -- (The school leadership library)
    Includes bibliographical references.
    ISBN 1-883001-47-1
    1. Educational counseling--United States.  2. Student assistance
programs--United States.  3. Student aspirations--United States.
4. Student activities--United States.  I. Worsham, Dode, 1943-   .
II. Title.  III. Series.
LB1027.5.W356  1998
371.4--dc21                                                  97-40110
                                                                  CIP
```

Production services provided by:
Bookwrights
1211 Courtland Drive
Raleigh, NC 27604

THE SCHOOL LEADERSHIP LIBRARY

INFORMATION COLLECTION
By Paula Short, Rick Jay Short, and Kenneth Brinson, Jr.

INSTRUCTION AND THE LEARNING ENVIRONMENT
by James W. Keefe and John M. Jenkins

INTERPERSONAL SENSITIVITY
by John R. Hoyle and Harry M. Crenshaw

JUDGMENT: MAKING THE RIGHT CALLS
By Jim Sweeney and Diana Bourisaw

LEADERSHIP: A RELEVANT AND REALISTIC
ROLE FOR PRINCIPALS
by Gary M. Crow, L. Joseph Matthews, and Lloyd E. McCleary

MOTIVATING OTHERS: CREATING THE CONDITIONS
by David P. Thompson

ORAL AND NONVERBAL EXPRESSION
by Ivan Muse

ORGANIZATIONAL OVERSIGHT:
PLANNING AND SCHEDULING FOR EFFECTIVENESS
by David A. Erlandson, Peggy L. Stark, and Sharon M. Ward

PROBLEM ANALYSIS: RESPONDING TO SCHOOL COMPLEXITY
By Charles M. Achilles, John S. Reynolds, and Susan H. Achilles

RESOURCE ALLOCATION
by M. Scott Norton and Larry K. Kelly

STUDENT GUIDANCE AND DEVELOPMENT
By Mary Ann Ward and Dode Worsham

WRITTEN EXPRESSION: THE PRINCIPAL'S SURVIVAL GUIDE
By India Podsen, Glenn Pethel, and John Waide

If you would like information about how to become a member of the School Leadership Library, please contact:

Eye On Education
6 Depot Way Suite 106
Larchmont, N.Y. 10538
(914) 833-0551 Phone   (914) 833-0761 Fax

ACKNOWLEDGMENTS

Recognizing that the purpose of this book is to provide practical assistance to principals in the area of student guidance by identifying examples of "best practice" programs, activities, and organizational structures, we turned to practitioners in the field for assistance. Throughout the book we have acknowledged many individuals and school staffs who have been willing to share with us, and in turn have allowed us to share with you, programs they have developed. We simply could not have written this book without their assistance.

We want to acknowledge a few professionals who allowed us time, resources, and the opportunity to ask lots of questions. These include Linda Baxter, Nila Marchant, Janice Connor, Francine Mayfield, Donna Barber, Ray Mathis, Peggy Moore, and Rita Arden. We would be remiss if we did not recognize Claudia Klausky, who turned sloppy sketches of forms and documents into professional-looking educational documents and was patient with us through many revisions. A special thank you to Al Wilson who enlisted us to write the book and remained our cheerleader and coach when our "real" job as principals kept us from making deadlines.

And finally, thanks to our staff at Katz-McMillan Cooperating Schools for being patient with us when we were not as accessible as usual because we were working on "the book." Most of all we thank our staff for consistently demonstrating that the ideas and principles outlined in this book are not "pie in the sky" idealism but can and do work when there is a commitment to implementing a program based on an understanding of child growth and development.

FOREWORD

The School Leadership Library was designed to show practicing and aspiring principals what they should know and be able to do to be effective leaders of their schools. The books in this series were written to answer the question, "How can we improve our schools by improving the effectiveness of our principals?"

Success in the principalship, like in other professions, requires mastery of a knowledge and skills base. One of the goals of the National Policy Board for Educational Administration (sponsored by NAESP, NASSP, AASA, ASCD, NCPEA, UCEA, and other professional organizations) was to define and organize that knowledge and skill base. The result of our efforts was the development of a set of 21 "domains," building blocks representing the core understanding and capabilities required of successful principals.

The 21 domains of knowledge and skills are organized under four broad areas: Functional, Programmatic, Interpersonal, and Contextual. They are as follows:

FUNCTIONAL DOMAINS
Leadership
Information Collection
Problem Analysis
Judgment
Organizational Oversight
Implementation
Delegation

PROGRAMMATIC DOMAINS
Instruction and the Learning
 Environment
Curriculum Design
Student Guidance and
 Development
Staff Development
Measurement and Evaluation
Resource Allocation

INTERPERSONAL DOMAINS
Motivating Others
Interpersonal Sensitivity
Oral and Nonverbal
  Expression
Written Expression

CONTEXTUAL DOMAINS
Philosophical and Cultural
  Values
Legal and Regulatory
  Applications
Policy and Political Influences
Public Relations

These domains are not discrete, separate entities. Rather, they evolved only for the purpose of providing manageable descriptions of essential content and practice so as to better understand the entire complex role of the principalship. Because human behavior comes in "bunches" rather than neat packages, the domains are also overlapping pieces of a complex puzzle. Consider the domains as converging streams of behavior that spill over one another's banks but that all contribute to the total reservoir of knowledge and skills required of today's principals.

The School Leadership Library was established by General Editors David Erlandson and Al Wilson to provide a broad examination of the content and skills in all of the domains. The authors of each volume in this series offer concrete and realistic illustrations and examples, along with reflective exercises. You will find their work to be of exceptional merit, illustrating with insight the depth and interconnectedness of the domains. This series provides the fullest, most contemporary, and most useful information available for the preparation and professional development of principals.

Scott Thomson
Executive Secretary
National Policy Board for
Educational Administration

PREFACE

Schools are more than buildings and walls, just as teaching and learning are more than textbooks, overhead projectors, and computers. When one thinks about an outstanding school it is not the institution that comes to mind but rather the interactions of the students, parents, teachers, and administrators. Volumes have been written about what makes up a good school. These characteristics include strong instructional leadership, high academic standards, a safe and orderly environment, and good home-school communications. While we would not deny that these descriptions are important and accurate, we believe there is yet another characteristic that sets some schools apart from others.

It is not a characteristic that is easily labeled. It is not something tangible but is rather an attitude on the part of the stakeholders that permeates the entire school environment and drives all decisions related to teaching and learning. What is this attitude that seems to set some schools apart? What sets the tone of the school from the start of the school year to the end? Why is it that when you walk into some schools you just know that exciting things are happening?

In this book, Mary Ann Ward and Dode Worsham have identified programs born out of a heartfelt desire on the part of school personnel to address the unique needs of students. These programs succeed when the administrator and staff apply their understanding of student growth and development and determine student needs through data analysis and ongoing evaluation. Programs propelled by these attitudes and vision meet with greater success than those created merely as a result of legislative mandates or as reactions to public demands.

In addition to describing programs for student growth and development which have been implemented at schools across the country, the authors also provide guidelines and suggestions for principals and prospective principals about how to utilize such programs. The authors also caution readers not to jump on any bandwagons. Before implementing any new program, it is important that you gather data from staff and parents related to the specific needs of your school, analyze the data carefully, and involve representatives from the staff and community in planning.

In Chapter 1, the authors provide a brief review of theories and principles related to child growth and development. Chapter 2 describeshow schools have used a variety of programs, including the organizational structure of schools and scheduling, to meet the social, emotional and academic needs of students. Chapters 3 and 4 deal primarily with the management of students through schoolwide behavior programs, including discipline, student recognition and incentive programs, and school-based counseling services. Within Chapter 5 the authors have identified and briefly described examples of extra curricular clubs and activities used at many schools to provide opportunities for students to develop leadership, interact with peers, gain first-hand experiences in a special interest area, and expand knowledge in a curricular area. Ways to involve parents in the school setting and suggestions related to parent communication are found in Chapter 6. Wherever possible the authors have provided samples of forms, letters, and other documents that have been created to support the various programs. These are found throughout the text and at the end of each chapter.

This practical resource guide will help administrators apply the principles of student growth and development to successfully implement programs to meet students' social, emotional, and academic needs. It provides the stimulus for principals and school staff to identify and create meaningful programs, keeping in mind the unique needs of students in an ever changing society.

David A. Erlandson
Alfred P. Wilson

ABOUT THE AUTHORS

Mary Ann Ward is the co-principal of Katz-McMillan Cooperating Schools, where she shares responsibilities with Dr. Dode Worsham. Mrs. Ward has taught various grade levels in the United States as well as overseas. Prior to becoming an administrator, she was a curriculum consultant in the areas of mathematics and science, a facilitator for Effective Schools and Mentoring and Coaching, and has designed and written pilot curriculum programs and workshops in the area of mathematics. Mrs. Ward has offered workshops and has presented at regional and national conferences. She is a founding member of the Nevada League of Professional Schools.

Dr. Dode Worsham is the co-principal of Katz-McMillan Cooperating Schools, a year-round elementary school in Las Vegas, Nevada. She has been an administrator for over ten years as well as an adjunct professor at the University of Nevada, Las Vegas, where she teaches a graduate-level reading course. She also teaches for NOVA University in the field of reading and school improvement. Dr. Worsham has been a public school teacher and a curriculum consultant for the Clark County School District. She has offered workshops, been a keynote speaker for Reading Conferences and is a founding member of the Nevada League of Professional Schools.

Table of Contents

1 **Principles of Student Growth and Development: Theories and Practices to Assist Educators** 1
   How Students Grow and Develop 2
      Jean Piaget 3
      Lev Vygotsky 5
      Erik Erikson 7
      Lawrence Kohlberg 8
   Practicality in the School 10
   Summary 11
   Follow-Up Activities 12

2 **Student Guidance: Utilizing Staff and Community to Meet Social and Academic Needs of Students** 13
   Meeting Student Needs: Peer Mediation, Adult Mentors, and Tutorial Programs 15
      Elementary School Peer Mediator Programs 15
      Secondary Peer Mediator Programs 17
      Adult Mentor Program 23
      Tutorial Programs 25
   Meeting Student Needs: A Team Approach 26
      Schoolwide Student Assistance Programs 27
   Meeting Student Needs: Organizational Change 30
      Multiage Classrooms 31
      Learning Communities 33
   Interdisciplinary Middle School Teaming 37
   Alternative High School Scheduling 39
      Magnet Schools 40
   Summary 41
   Follow-Up Activities 42
   Resources 43
   Documents 45

TABLE OF CONTENTS　　　　　　　　　　　　　　　　　　　　xi

3　STUDENT GUIDANCE: DEVELOPING STUDENT SOCIAL
　　RESPONSIBILITY 57
　　　STUDENT INCENTIVE PROGRAMS 57
　　　　ELEMENTARY INCENTIVES 58
　　　　MIDDLE SCHOOL/JUNIOR HIGH/HIGH SCHOOL
　　　　　INCENTIVES 64
　　　SCHOOLWIDE DISCIPLINE PROGRAMS 65
　　　　ADDITIONAL RESOURCES 72
　　　SUMMARY 73
　　　FOLLOW-UP ACTIVITIES 73
　　　RESOURCES 74
　　　DOCUMENTS 75

4　STUDENT GUIDANCE: GUIDANCE AND
　　COUNSELING SERVICES 99
　　　SCHOOL-BASED GUIDANCE AND COUNSELING
　　　　PROGRAMS 100
　　　　ROLE OF THE ELEMENTARY SCHOOL COUNSELOR 102
　　　　ROLE OF THE MIDDLE SCHOOL COUNSELOR 102
　　　　ROLE OF THE SENIOR HIGH SCHOOL COUNSELOR 103
　　　　ADVANTAGES OF SCHOOL-BASED GUIDANCE AND
　　　　　COUNSELING PROGRAMS 104
　　　　INDIVIDUAL/GROUP GUIDANCE AND COUNSELING 108
　　　　REFERRING STUDENTS FOR COUNSELING SERVICES 109
　　　SCHOOLS WITHOUT A COUNSELOR 109
　　　PARENT EDUCATION CLASSES 114
　　　SUMMARY 115
　　　FOLLOW-UP ACTIVITIES 116
　　　RESOURCES 116
　　　DOCUMENTS 120

5　STUDENT GUIDANCE: STUDENT ACTIVITY PROGRAMS 125
　　　ELEMENTARY CLUBS AND ORGANIZATIONS 127
　　　SECONDARY SCHOOL CLUBS AND ORGANIZATIONS 128
　　　　CLUBS/ORGANIZATIONS 129
　　　　PERFORMING GROUPS 131
　　　　ATHLETIC PROGRAMS 132

	Summary	132
	Follow-Up Activities	133
	Resources	133
6	Student Guidance: Parents In Partnership With Schools	135
	Parent Involvement in Planning	137
	Communication With Parents	138
	Schoolwide Communication	139
	Communication About Student Progress	140
	Parent Network/Support Groups	143
	Parents as Instructional Partners	144
	Art Docent Program	144
	Student Publishing Center	144
	Enlisting Parent Volunteers	146
	Summary	147
	Follow-Up Activities	147
	Resources	148
	Documents	150
7	Selected References	163

1

PRINCIPLES OF STUDENT GROWTH AND DEVELOPMENT: THEORIES AND PRACTICES TO ASSIST EDUCATORS

The morning has been fairly quiet, just the usual problems dealing with a shortage of substitutes, a fight on bus #3, a seemingly endless line of staff who want to know if you have "gotta minute," and the everyday dealings with students ranging from a pushing contest to a fourth grade student ditching class. Lunch is now over and you settle down to begin the paperwork that has been piling up on your desk when you hear via the intercom, "Miguel has left room 41, hitting a student, and flinging a desk across the room as he left." You immediately begin mentally to sort through the alternatives available to you and think where you might begin to look for him. As you grab the two-way radio and head down the hallway, you reflect on the amount of time you and the staff have spent putting in place a plan to address Miguel's volatile behavior. You feel a sense of failure that the efforts have met with little success. This is not the first time you have encountered Miguel nor will it be the last. Once Miguel is found and has calmed down, he will once more become the charmer everyone enjoys. Promises of improved behavior will be made, but you know, because of past experiences with Miguel, that these promises will not be kept.

As administrators all of us have dealt with similar situations and have likely been involved in even more serious scenarios. Children are coming to our schools with various factors altering their lives. We live in a society with more single parents than ever before, who often are working at two jobs to make ends meet. Dysfunctional families, custody battles, emotional problems, children who are abused and neglected, and large class sizes all contribute to the growing problems that we often find in our schools. We feel that before we can tackle specific problems or solutions to some of these issues, we need to revisit some of the principles of student growth and development. It is the intent of this book to provide principals and other school administrators with user-friendly ideas and strategies related to meeting the developmental needs of students in the school setting, including a review of many successful programs that have been put in place at schools across the country.

While our emphasis is not on theory but rather on practical suggestions, it has helped us to rethink and reflect on some of the theories developed by prominent thinkers regarding how children develop. Revisiting Child Development 101 from time to time helps both administrators and teachers look for solutions based on the emotional, social, and physical needs of students.

HOW STUDENTS GROW AND DEVELOP

Kurt Lewin (1931), a behaviorist scientist, stated, "Human behavior is the product of the interaction between the growing human organism and its environment." Even though this was written more than sixty years ago, we think that it continues to be appropriate now and lends itself to this section on how we might identify and implement effective programs that meet the instructional and behavioral needs of students. Jean Piaget, Lev Vygotsky, Erik Erikson, and Lawrence Kohlberg have greatly influenced our understanding of how children develop cognitively, socially, and morally. Some of their findings, hopefully, will assist us in making decisions related to student guidance and development.

JEAN PIAGET

Piaget's work describing the developmental stages of cognitive growth is part of every teacher's course work and has more recently been revisited by Ed Labinowicz (1985). Each stage is characterized by the emerging of new abilities that result in differences in how children think. Table 1.1 describes Piaget's Four Stages of Cognitive Development, which could be used by administrators and teachers not only to look at the emotional well-being of students but also to assist them in assigning the curriculum that is appropriate to the level of the child.

Piaget's theory has had a major impact on practices and methodologies in education. Such practices and methodologies focus on:

- the use of developmentally appropriate instructional practices
- actively involving children in learning activities
- encouraging discovery through the child's spontaneous interactions with the environment
- the acceptance of individual differences in the developmental process

Much has been written about the extent to which Piaget's findings affect the curriculum in schools and how children actually learn.

Piaget not only studied the cognitive development of children but he also studied the social and moral development of humans. In his theory of moral development, Piaget (1964) indicated that morality does not exist before the age of six, so for children of this age, no true rules exist. Piaget discovered that children at age two played with an object without regard to rules or purpose. Between the ages of two and six, children begin to be aware of rules, but still do not see the need or purpose for them. How might this directly impact early childhood programs

TABLE 1.1
FOUR STAGES OF COGNITIVE DEVELOPMENT

AGE	STAGE	DEVELOPMENT
Birth to 2 years	Sensorimotor (learning about surroundings using senses & motor skills)	Trial and error learning, concept of object permanence, beginning of thinking and planning behavior
2 years to 7 years	Preoperational (learning mentally to represent things)	Ability to use symbols to represent objects, thinking is egocentric and centered on one dimension, lack of reversibility and conservation
7 years to 11 years	Concrete operational (developing skills of logical reasoning and conversation)	Concept of seriation, ability to conserve, class inclusion, solving problems as long as they involve objects and situations that are familiar, abstract thinking not in place
11 years to adults	Formal operation (dealing abstractly with hypothetical situations and reasons)	Thinks abstractly, testing hypothesis about situations and conditions, systematic experimentation, higher-level thinking skills

at your school? Does the curriculum need to reflect this development, and knowing this, how do you deal with a preschooler who does not appear to be able to follow the rules?

From the ages of six to ten, children begin to acknowledge the existence of rules but are inconsistent in their thinking. It is during this stage that children see rules as imposed by a higher authority and view rules as unchangeable. They do not view rules as arbitrary and something that could be decided on together. How many times during lunch duty do you hear teachers/staff tell students of this age to come to an agreement about the game or make a decision as to how the game will be played? Is this appropriate? When we as administrators are dealing with disciplinary actions, for example, when students break a rule, how do we incorporate this idea into the consequence or the way we handle the situation?

Around ten to twelve years of age, when children are transitioning from the concrete operational stage to the formal operational stage, they begin to use and follow rules conscientiously. At this age, Piaget found that children are able to play a game following the same set of rules. They are able to understand that rules exist to give a game or situation direction and to minimize disruptions. This, then, may have ramifications for middle schools that deal primarily with children from the ages of eleven to thirteen.

Because of the changes that take place in understanding and applying rules, Piaget identified two stages of moral development: heteronomous morality and autonomous morality. Heteronomous morality is defined as the stage of moral realism or the morality of constraint and is considered to be the first stage of moral development. It is at this stage that persons in authority generally tell children what to do and what not to do. Children learn that violation of these rules bring automatic consequences, in other words, "the bad guys will get theirs."

In the next stage, autonomous morality, or morality by cooperation, the interaction with others causes children to change their ideas about rules and morality. Through peer interaction and cooperation children come to realize that rules are not always clearly defined and that consequences for breaking the rules often vary according to the circumstances.

LEV VYGOTSKY

Lev Vygotsky's work, originally written in Russian, has been receiving more attention since being translated into English and is now mentioned in reading methods courses as it applies to the teaching of reading. His work addresses areas of growth and development somewhat differently than Piaget. Vygotsky was a Russian psychologist living about the same time as Piaget who challenged Piaget's premise that the best way to observe children's thinking processes was to observed them in isolation

(1978, p. 79). He felt it far more valuable to observe and study children as they interacted with each other and with adults. Vygotsky theorized that the thinking abilities of children develop primarily as an outcome of attempting to communicate with other human beings, and this was best determined when a child was interacting with adults or advanced peers. Vygotsky placed a heavy emphasis on the importance of social learning and the internalization of culture and social relationships as related to the development of mental processes. Cultural influences, according to Vygotsky, are society's way of providing the child with goals and the structured methods needed to achieve these goals.

Vygotsky is perhaps best known for his work related to the zone of proximal development. Once again, he believed that it was important to look at the cognitive and social development of a child, not in isolation, but in light of the child's interaction with another person. Trudge (1990) states that according to Vygotsky, a child has both an actual developmental level, which can be assessed by testing the child individually, and a potential developmental level, which can be assessed by examining learning that occurs when the child is problem solving under the guidance of an adult or is working in collaboration with more capable peers.

> The zone of proximal development defines those functions that have not yet matured but are in the process of maturation, functions that will mature tomorrow but are currently in an embryonic state. These functions could be termed the "bud" or "flowers" of development rather than the "fruits" of development. (1978, p. 86)

Vygotsky's work related to the zone of proximal development and cultural influences has implications for teachers and administrators in establishing programs that provide a support system for students as they are constructing their own understanding of their world.

As administrators, we have found that many of our veteran teachers are not familiar with the work of Vygotsky. His work has implications for many of the programs being used in schools such as peer tutoring, cooperative group work, and schoolwide discipline/behavior programs. An excellent resource to help both administrators and teachers understand the educational implication of Vygotsky's is *Vygotsky and Education*.

ERIK ERIKSON

Erik Erikson postulated eight stages of personal and social development, six of which pertain to school-age children. He believed that people go through these eight psychosocial stages in their lives, with crises or critical issues that need to be resolved at each stage. According to Erikson, if people do not resolve these crises, they will continue to deal with them throughout their lives. The six stages that pertain to school-age students are identified in Table 1.2.

TABLE 1.2
ERIKSON'S STAGES OF PERSONAL AND SOCIAL DEVELOPMENT

AGE	STAGE	DESCRIPTOR
1. Birth to 18 months	Trust vs. Mistrust	Goal is to develop a basic trust in the world
2. 18 months to 3 years	Autonomy vs. Doubt	Ability to do things by oneself, beginning sense of autonomy
3. 3 to 6 years	Initiative vs. Guilt	Increasing aggression in exploration in both social and physical world
4. 6 to 12 years	Industry vs. Inferiority	Sense of industry, want to make things, good feelings about oneself
5. 12 to 18 years	Identity vs. Role Confusion	Time of change, Who am I? turning away from parents
6. Young adulthood	Intimacy vs. Isolation	Losing and finding oneself in another

According to Erikson (1963), the school plays a central role for children during the industry versus inferiority stage and the identity versus role confusion stage. During the elementary years, it is important to be aware that students are trying hard to maintain a positive self-concept and to view themselves as capable and valuable individuals. The school, therefore, is the place where success and failure are defined. Erikson (1963) describes the school as the logical setting for providing students with the tools they need to participate in society. A question that we need to ask ourselves is, What opportunities, at the school level, are being provided for students to develop the necessary skills to function in today's society?

The identity versus role confusion stage is where adolescents are trying to break away from parental control and establish themselves as independent persons. Many times the teacher is seen in the same light as the parent, so students during this stage often reject the teacher's authority as much as they do that of their parents.

During adolescence, children want to be treated as adults. Erikson found that if adolescents are treated this way, they are more likely to respond with adultlike behaviors. They do not want to be referred to or treated as children, and they do not want to be belittled or humiliated in front of their peers. Explicit expectations and rules, with clearly defined consequences for achieving or failing, are needed for adolescence. Providing opportunities for students at this stage to work in cooperative groups is effective because the opinion and influence of the peer group are so powerful. At the high school level, forming clubs where students are actively involved in making decisions and providing leadership (outlined in Chapter 5) fits in nicely with Erikson's theory.

LAWRENCE KOHLBERG

The last theorist that we are going to review is Lawrence Kohlberg, who also studied the moral development of children. He studied how children responded to a series of some structured situations or moral dilemmas, and as a result identified six stages of moral judgment or reasoning (Slavin, 1994, p. 61).

The six stages are divided into three levels: preconventional, conventional, and postconventional (Table 1.3).

TABLE 1.3
KOLHBERG'S STAGES OF MORAL REASONING

LEVEL	PRECONVENTIONAL	
	Stage 1:	Children simply obey authority figures to avoid punishment
	Stage 2:	Children begin to weigh interests of all parties when making moral judgment, however, they still look out for themselves
LEVEL	**CONVENTIONAL**	
	Stage 3:	Undoubting belief in golden rule, people begin considering feelings of others when making moral decisions
	Stage 4:	Laws/Rules are followed without question and breaking law cannot be justified
LEVEL	**POSTCONVENTIONAL**	
	Stage 5:	Laws are necessary to preserve social order and ensure rights of all
	Stage 6:	Ethical principles are self-chosen and based on abstract concepts

Each stage is more complex and sophisticated than the previous one, with individuals proceeding through them in the same order. Similar to Piaget's developmental stages, moving from one stage to the other does not occur at exactly the same time or in the same way for each child; however, most children have passed from the preconventional to the conventional level by about the age of nine.

Kohlberg's preconventional level of morality corresponds to Piaget's heteronomous morality stage. Children obey authority figures in order to avoid punishment. In stage two, children are aware of the interests of others but primarily look out for themselves.

The conventional level of morality corresponds to Piaget's autonomous morality stage, with children beginning to consider the feelings of others when making moral decisions. During stage four, society's rules and laws replace those of the peer groups. Generally, children follow the rules without question, and breaking a rule is never okay.

Kohlberg believed that only about 25 percent of all adults ever reach the postconventional stage. This stage deals with the idea that laws are seen as necessary to preserve the social order and to provide for the basic rights of life and liberty (Slavin, 1994, p. 62).

Kohlberg believed that a teacher could assist in advancing a child's level of moral reasoning by providing opportunities to discuss and deal with issues related to social responsibility and ethics, particularly as related to the classroom or school setting. The idea of classroom meetings and open debates about issues are suggestions that administrators might give classroom teachers who are experiencing frustration in dealing with students. The most serious limitation to applying Kohlberg's theory to the school setting is that it deals with moral reasoning rather than actual behaviors.

PRACTICALITY IN THE SCHOOL

Now that we have revisited several of the theories of student growth and development, how can we use this knowledge to help us with a Miguel or with another student that a teacher brings to us? We have found that providing staff members with an overview of these theories, discussing the ramifications of each, and setting up situations in which teachers can work together to plan a course of action, assists them in developing effective programs. Asking teachers to work through the different theories with a particular student in mind empowers them to use their expertise, knowledge, and training in dealing with the student.

SUMMARY

Examining theories of student growth and development will shed some light on the developmental stages of students. By reviewing several different theories, we feel that we can better understand our students. By sharing this information with teachers, we help them have a better understanding of their complex job when dealing with the developmental levels of students. We have not only been given the responsibility of educating children, we have also been charged with helping them come to grips with their own growth and development.

The following chapters are meant to be a practical guide for developing and maintaining a school atmosphere that is conducive to learning, while promoting good decision making and creating support programs that develop social awareness as well as academic success. The focus will be on:

- programs and models designed to meet the individual academic, social, and behavioral needs of students
- utilization of staff to provide appropriate guidance and activity programs, including student recognition, incentives, and student discipline
- descriptors of student guidance and counseling programs, K–12
- student intracurricular and extracurricular activities that promote student responsibility
- home–school relationships to support student growth and development

In professional journals there are articles and book reviews that describe effective programs that are developed to promote and support student growth and development academically, socially, and behaviorally. The programs identified and described in the following pages reflect a portion of those available or those that have been implemented and found to be effective. Where possible, resource information has been provided so that readers may request additional information regarding programs and activities.

FOLLOW-UP ACTIVITIES

1. Imagine a situation where a teacher asks you as the administrator to help her with a student who does not want to follow the rules that she has set for her class. How would you use the information in this chapter to assist her? What questions would you want to ask her in order to understand where this student is developmentally?

2. As a principal, you want to provide your teachers with information regarding the different theories pertaining to student growth and development during the next staff meeting. You have approximately 30 minutes and want the teachers to leave the meeting with something they can use in their classrooms. Where would you start? How would you relate this to their everyday experiences?

3. A parent comes to you asking you to explain why working in groups at the middle school level is necessary in her son's classroom. How would you respond in light of the different theories of student growth and development?

2

Student Guidance: Utilizing Staff and Community to Meet Social and Academic Needs of Students

The bell just rang announcing the end of another school day! You know you must rush out to bus duty, see Mrs. Smith about the assembly schedule before she leaves for the day, deal with a parent who is waiting in the office with a concern about the PTA fund raiser, call a parent about an ongoing discipline problem with a student in fifth grade, meet with the student intervention team about retention policies, and send in the budget report that is due in the superintendent's office by 4:00 p.m. (Hooray for FAX machines!) Just as you begin to tackle these tasks the PTA president knocks on your door and reminds you that she must have your article for the newsletter immediately. She also gently reminds you that it was due two days ago. It's now 6:00 p.m. and you're feeling pretty good because you've managed to get it all done and you can call it quits for the day when you notice that your secretary has strategically placed on your desk the mail you've not gone through in several days.

In the deluge of mail you find many flyers, advertisements, and commercial programs that promise to answer all the issues you've dealt with throughout the day, and specifically in the last two hours. How to Utilize Parents on the Playground, computer software for Time Management and Budget, prewritten principal newsletter articles on every topic you can imagine, reading and mathematics programs designed to meet the needs of the at-risk student, the English Second Language student, the gifted student, Discipline Programs That Really Work, and the list goes on.

In the first chapter we discussed the importance of a school administrator having a good understanding of student growth and development, and the need for an administrator to be able to apply that understanding to decisions regarding programs being implemented at the school. A vast number of new programs surface and are introduced to educators each year claiming great success in addressing behavioral and academic needs of students. As educators we are constantly looking for ways to improve the existing educational environment, therefore we are easy prey for advertising that promises a quick fix or a sure thing. Individual schools and school districts frequently fall into the trap of purchasing or adopting programs just because the program has worked in another setting.

A variety of programs and models will be described in this chapter that are being used in elementary and secondary schools to address the individual needs of students in social, behavioral, and academic realms. However, before any new program is implemented it is critical that school personnel conduct an assessment of current conditions at the school in order to have a clear understanding of actual need. This can be accomplished through school-developed staff and parent surveys, commercially developed surveys, and/or brainstorming and dialogue sessions with representatives from all areas of the community.

The administrator must assume leadership in this area and work closely with staff and parents to establish a vision for the school and identify specific goals. If one of the goals is to provide programs that address the individual needs of students, the stakeholders of the school community must come to an understanding of what is actually meant by the phrase "meeting the needs of individual students." Once there is a common understanding of terms and a clear vision has been established, school personnel are ready to develop and put in place an action plan. Frequently this calls for reviewing strategies and programs that have been used in other settings. It is important, however, to remember that most successful programs are those developed by on-site staff based on the specific needs of the school, with consideration given to developmental theory and research based "best practice."

MEETING STUDENT NEEDS: PEER MEDIATION, ADULT MENTORS, AND TUTORIAL PROGRAMS

Many schools, both elementary and secondary, have developed and successfully implemented schoolwide student mediator and tutoring programs in an attempt to meet the social and academic needs of students. In thinking about what might be helpful in assisting administrators in this area we have chosen to describe specific mediator and/or tutoring programs that have been developed on-site by individual schools. We also reference two commercial peer mediator programs.

ELEMENTARY SCHOOL PEER MEDIATOR PROGRAMS

Many discipline problems at the elementary school level occur on the playground before school or during recess times. Most incidents include such minor problems as name calling, cutting or pushing in line, disagreement over the score of a game, or fair distribution of playground equipment. A peer mediation program where students are trained to assist in resolving these kinds of problems has proven successful in some elementary schools.

One such program was developed by Dr. Peggy Moore, principal of the James I. Gibson Elementary School in Henderson, Nevada. Dr. Moore states, "Our students are learning that issues can be resolved more effectively by talking them out than by fighting. It has been thrilling to watch students who have had several opportunities to be mediators improve their problem solving skills as they move from grade level to grade level."

At Gibson Elementary each teacher identifies two students every two weeks to serve as peer mediators. Peer mediators receive training in how to solve problems on the playground. According to Dr. Moore (Cahoon, 1987/1988), students who serve as mediators learn valuable problem-solving skills, to think logically about processing information presented to them, to see issues impartially, and to advise without censoring. Student mediators:

- serve as peer models
- keep an eye out for any problems that might be brewing
- stop what they are doing to solve a problem
- ask one person to talk at a time
- ask the people to use soft voices
- listen to both sides
- ask each person what it is that he or she wants the other person to stop doing
- ask each person if he or she is able to stop doing those things
- suggest that they stop doing those things
- ask the students to apologize and shake hands
- ask the students if the problem has been solved, or if it should be referred to an adult
- if the problem has not been solved, take it to an adult
- notice if a serious problem is brewing and alert an adult

Student mediators DO NOT:

- issue citations, police or patrol
- tattle
- scold or demand
- pass judgment
- force themselves on others
- get in the middle of a fight
- ignore people who are having a problem

A peer mediator program provides the opportunity for students to become active participants in creating a safe learning environment. The staff at Gibson Elementary created a variety of documents that can be used in implementing a peer mediator program at the elementary level. Figure 2.1 is a copy of a letter sent to all students who are selected as peer mediators. Figure 2.2, Mediator Musts, outlines what is covered at the training for mediators, and Figure 2.3 is the Mediator's Covenant which is signed by all mediators. For further information regarding the peer mediator program at James I. Gibson Elementary, contact:

> Dr. Peggy Moore
> James I. Gibson Elementary School
> 271 Leisure Circle
> Henderson, Nevada 89104
> 702-799-8730

SECONDARY PEER MEDIATION PROGRAMS

In an attempt to meet individual student needs and address problems unique to adolescence in grades 6 through 12, many secondary schools have also successfully implemented peer mediation programs. Such programs are designed to identify and train selected student helpers to assist peers in finding solutions to problems and to know where to go for help. The basic concept of such mediation programs is students helping students. It is built on the premise that students are more likely to take advice from their friends than from anyone else and that with appropriate training many students can assist in providing reliable and helpful information to peers in need of assistance.

Titles such as Peer Mediators, Student Helpers, Peer Assistants, Natural Helpers, Student Assistance Program, and Peer Facilitators are used in the many peer mediation programs that have been developed and are being used in schools. While programs vary in depth and sophistication of training and implementation, most have the following commonalities:

- ♦ Students are identified and selected to participate in the peer mediation program

Figure 2.1 Letter to Peer Mediators

Date

Dear Mediator,

Congratulations! You have been selected to participate in our peer mediation program. As a mediator, you will be working with the staff and administrators to create a wonderful school environment where problems are solved the right way, without arguing and fighting. Learning to solve problems in this way will be of great help to you throughout your life.

Being a mediator is a real responsibility. When individuals are involved in a conflict and cannot solve the problem themselves, they will come to you so you can help them talk out the problem and decide on a solution. While you are helping students solve problems, you are to use the sheet entitled Mediator Musts to guide you. Always remember how important it is to stop playing and help those in need. Also remember you do not always have to wait for problems to come to you; you can keep your eyes and ears open so you can (1) spot situations that may lead to problems and (2) see if anyone seems sad and may need a friend.

Please know your teachers and I appreciate your willingness to help your friends at _____ Elementary School be safe and happy. Thanks to people like you, there are lots of smiling faces on our campus!
Again, congratulations!

Sincerely,

Principal

FIGURE 2.2 MEDIATOR MUSTS

IF YOU SEE A PROBLEM OR IF SOMEONE COMES TO YOU WITH A PROBLEM, YOU MUST:
1. Realize how important the mediator job is.
2. Stop playing so you can help those who have a problem.
3. Ask each person involved in the problem these questions:
   a. What is the problem?
   b. What do you want the other person to stop doing?
   c. Can you stop being unkind?
   d. Is the problem over?
4. Be kind and always set a good example.
5. Wear your hat or strap because orange is our safety color. Remember to take good care of it.
6. As you talk with students, be sure you:
   a. do not take sides. Treat everyone as equals.
   b. ask one person to speak at a time.
   c. ask the students to use soft voices.
   d. use a polite tone of voice.
   e. politely ask those who may be watching to leave or, if necessary, move to a different area to talk.
   f. ask the students to say they are sorry.
   g. let the principal know how you solved a problem so she can thank you for your hard work.
   h. SEEK ADULT HELP IF YOU FEEL A PROBLEM IS NOT OVER.
7. Remember you should not:
   a. get in the middle of a fight. Get adult help if you see a fight underway.
   b. be bossy or scold the student.
   c. ignore people who have a problem.

FIGURE 2.2 MEDIATOR MUSTS CONT'D

8. In the lunchroom, you are asked to:
   a. pick your spot and stand at the end of your table.
   b. always keep your eyes open for students who may want to be dismissed.
   c. go to the student who wants to be dismissed and check the floor and table. Do not dismiss students by simply signaling for them to leave.
   d. clean any mess that may have been left behind.
   e. remain at your station for 15 minutes.
   f. report for duty every day for two weeks.
   g. ask permission to leave.

9. On the playground, you should:
   a. keep your eyes and ears open so you can help students before they become sad or upset.
   b. keep an eye out for strangers. Let an adult know if you see someone who seems suspicious.
   c. stop playing when someone comes to you for help.
   d. get a pass from an adult so you can bring an injured child to the office.
   e. always remember you are there to help others.

10. In your classroom, you are asked to:
    a. be a FIRST FRIEND to new students, take them on a tour of the building, introduce them to the principal, and escort them to the library, lunchroom, etc.
    b. greet any visitors who enter your room.

FIGURE 2.3 MEDIATOR'S COVENANT

AS A MEDIATOR I PROMISE TO:

____ listen to both sides

____ ask the four problem-solving questions

____ stop playing in order to help others

____ keep an eye out for potential problems

____ be a new student's first friend

____ take a new student on a tour of the building

____ welcome visitors to our room

____ see that my lunch table is clean

____ see that the floor under my lunch table is clean

____ help anyone who is hurt or sad

____ behave at all times in a kind manner

____ be fair and honest

_____

Student's Signature

- Program goals are outlined and defined for students and staff
- Ongoing training is provided for students participating in the peer mediation program
- Student roles are identified and frequently include:
  - assisting friends with problems
  - recognizing when a peer is having a serious problem related to depression, chemical dependency or abuse, and referring them to trained helping resources
  - participating in a support group of other peer mediators to discuss issues and problems
  - working in the dean's/counselor's office as a trained problem solver
  - making counselors or other staff aware when a student has experienced a family change, such as death or divorce
  - observing students who are being pressured by peers to get involved in illegal activities and offering assistance
  - teaching skills to younger students
  - listening and providing a sympathetic ear to someone who is having trouble with relationships
  - assisting students new to the school

The American School Counselor Association has recognized the concept of peer mediation as a means of assisting students in accessing the support and help they need in dealing with problems. Peervention and Natural Helpers are two commercial peer mediation programs that are being used in some schools. For further information contact:

Peervention
Training Peer Facilitators for Prevention Education
Robert D. Myrick, Ph.D., and Betsy E. Folk, Ph.D.
Educational Media Corporation
Box 21311
Minneapolis, MN 55421-0311

Natural Helpers
Roberts, Fitzmahan & Associates, Inc.
9131 California Ave, SW
Seattle, WA 98136
206-932-8409

ADULT MENTOR PROGRAM

An Adult Mentor Program is another avenue schools are using to provide support and assistance to at-risk students who are experiencing personal and academic problems in school. Adult staff volunteers within the school setting or community are enlisted to participate in the program. The mentors receive training and meet together periodically to share ideas on how to build personal relationships with these at-risk students.

The goal of the program is for adult mentors to develop genuine, supportive, trustworthy rapport with the students. Students are recommended for the program by any staff person. Students are introduced to the Mentor Program through a friendly, informal conference, and then are carefully matched up with mentors. The mentors develop positive relationships with students by assisting them in establishing goals and praising their accomplishments. Students may participate in a one-on-one weekly conference with mentors, as well as other activities such as having lunch together, attending a school function, and informal phone calls.

Such a program was implemented at Green Valley High School, Henderson, Nevada, under the direction of Ms. Janice Connor, Dean of Students. Ms. Connor reports that through participation in the Gator Mentor Program many students demonstrated improved interpersonal and problem-solving skills, exhibited more appropriate school behavior, and attended school more regularly. Parents of students who participated in the program expressed gratitude for the added support provided by the school and indicated they felt their child greatly benefited from the program.

The following documents were created by Ms. Connor for the program at Green Valley High School and appear at the end of this chapter.

Document 2.1   Mentor Program Procedures: general program procedures distributed to adult mentors
Document 2.2   Mentor Program Guidelines: expectancies for adult mentors who participate in the program
Document 2.3   Mentor Program Questionnaire: to be completed by the adult mentor
Document 2.4   Student Progress Questionnaire: to be completed by the adult mentor
Document 2.5   Mentor Program Contact/Conference Log
Document 2.6   Parent Letter

Dallas Independent School District developed and implemented an adult mentor program in 1994 at selected middle schools, involving members of the community through the North Dallas Chamber of Commerce reaching out to small as well as large businesses. The goal of the first year was to enlist and train ten adult mentors to work with identified at-risk middle school students. By the end of the first year sixty-two adult mentors had become involved in the program with more than sixty-two middle school students. The Dallas program is based on the National Association of Partners in Education's *School-Based Mentoring Programs*. According to the program description, "mentoring is a one-on-one relationship over a prolonged period of time between a youth and an adult who provides support, guidance, and concrete help." The Dallas program seeks to provide a combination of mentor/tutor in order to infuse learning and reinforcement into the relationship as needed to promote academic achievement. As in other adult mentor programs, specific guidelines are established regarding mentoring expectations and a significant amount of time is dedicated to the training of mentors.

Rosemary Morice, Specialist in Community Relations for the Dallas Public Schools, indicated the program had met with great success and there were plans to expand the program to include special guest speakers and field trips to work sites for the students. For further information regarding this program contact

Rosemary Morice, Dallas Public Schools, 3700 Ross Avenue, Box 40, Dallas, Texas 75204, Phone: 214-989-8328.

TUTORIAL PROGRAMS

The instructional program of the one-room school house depended on older students assisting with the instruction of younger students. As schools consolidated and school facilities were built to accommodate students being organized by grade level, the idea of "big kids" helping "little kids" was not used as extensively. Later in this chapter the organization of multi-age classrooms and the concept of Learning Communities will be discussed as some educators are revisiting the benefits of the one-room schoolhouse concept in meeting individual needs of students. In addition to these kinds of programs, many schools use a variety of tutorial programs built around the belief that both the tutor and the one being tutored benefit from such programs.

Senior Adult Tutors. Senior adults volunteering to work with students in elementary schools has met with great success in many communities. Some schools have established a special room for the senior adult tutors at the school in order to recognize the contribution they are making to students at the school. Senior adults contribute in a variety of ways, which include reading to students, listening to students read, escorting students to special classes, assisting students on the playground and in the lunchroom, and sometimes being a surrogate grandparent to a young child whose grandparents are not living or live far away.

Cross Grade Level Tutoring. Tutoring programs at the elementary school level often include upper grade level classes working regularly with lower grade level classes. Many schools have found such programs to be quite successful, particularly in the areas of language arts and mathematics. Student tutoring can be as simple as an older student reading to or with a younger student on a one-to-one basis or an entire fifth grade class adopting a second grade class to assist in writing process instruction. Often such pairings have benefits beyond the classrooms and instructional program. Schools that have used cross-age tutoring report an increased support system for young students on the playground because the older students feel a sense of responsibility for their welfare and safety.

A program developed by a high school teacher and elementary special education teacher has met with considerable success in the Clark County School District, Las Vegas, Nevada. The program, Helping You-Helping Me, is a student-based, student-generated tutorial program, matching motivated high school students with elementary students who need instructional assistance. The program was developed in 1988 by Bobby Cartwright and Donna Barber and has been recognized by Nevada PTA as an exemplary tutorial program.

For further information regarding this program you may contact:

Ms. Donna Barber
c/o A Barber-Cartwright Production
1121 Passion Flower Circle
Las Vegas, NV 89108
702-647-2746

MEETING STUDENT NEEDS: A TEAM APPROACH

School administrators deal on a daily basis with the increasing demands and guidelines associated with students receiving services through special education, compensatory education, and second language programs. Working through all the bureaucratic red tape is sometimes frustrating, but an even greater frustration is recognizing there are many students who are in need of special assistance but do not fit the guidelines to receive any extra services. The number of students being diagnosed ADHD/ADD is increasing at an alarming rate, and students with severe physical disabilities and severe learning disabilities are being included more and more in regular classrooms.

Handling special education issues often requires an inordinate amount of time on the part of the school administrator. Deciding who should be tested, determining priority in testing, making retention decisions, ensuring that appropriate intervention strategies have been implemented, participating in the writing of Individual Education Plans (IEPs), and making sure the school is in compliance with federal and state mandates are just some of the issues that school administrators deal with in order to meet individual needs of students. Administrators can no longer afford to assume full responsibility for making these decisions, the risks are too high. How can administrators meet these demands?

A growing number of schools and school districts have implemented a site-based team approach to deal with the scope of special needs issues at the school level. Teams of teachers and other support staff are being organized and trained to provide additional assistance to students at the school site. These teams often bear a name that denotes the scope of their responsibility, names such as Student Intervention Team, Student Assistance Team, Schoolwide Assistance Team, HELP Team, Pupil Assistance Team, Prereferral Team, and Teachers Assisting Teachers.

SCHOOLWIDE STUDENT ASSISTANCE PROGRAMS

Student assistance or intervention programs are established at many schools, both elementary and secondary, in an attempt to assist teachers in working with students who demonstrate academic or behavior concerns who may or may not qualify for services through special education. Sometimes these programs are viewed as prereferral interventions for special education, but in many cases these programs provide a systematic means for teachers working with other teachers to prevent student failure through early detection and remediation.

Many schools effectively use building-level pupil assistance teams consisting of adults at the school to provide assistance to regular classroom teachers to work with at-risk students. These assistance teams are usually made up of veteran teachers who foster the idea that teachers assisting teachers is more effective and meaningful than depending on an outside expert to come in and fix the problem at the school site.

There are a variety of models developed by school districts, state departments, and commercial publishers that set guidelines for establishing site-based pupil assistance teams. While models vary somewhat in design and scope, most contain the following commonalities:

1. A team of teachers and other staff members who systematically work together to address the academic and behavioral needs of students by providing assistance and support to the regular classroom teacher. (The teams primarily consist of regular education teachers but may include ancillary staff such as the school psychologist, nurse, counselor, speech therapist, and administrator.)
2. A referral or request for assistance procedure that teachers use to access the help and support of the team (Document 2.7).
3. A variety of diagnostic or screening tools used by the team to assist in determining specific areas of concern and identifying possible causes for problem areas. (Sometimes these tools are developed by the team, but more often teams use well-recognized commercial assessment measures.)
4. The identification of effective strategies in addressing both academic and behavioral problems.
5. Documentation and record keeping maintained to ensure accountability and follow-through. (Without a built-in plan for recording what is to be done, when it is to be done and who will do it, teams often meet and discuss issues related to student problems but rarely accomplish very much. When this occurs teams are viewed as ineffective and after a period of time cease to exist. Documents 2.8 and 2.9 are samples of documentation and record-keeping forms that may be used by the team to monitor requests for assistance and record action plans.)
6. Inservice training for the Student Assistance Team, as well as the full staff. (This is an important component if the program is be implemented effectively. Parents must be made aware of such a program and how it differs from special education. Document 2.10 is a letter that may be sent to parents concerning referral of their child to the assistance team. Document

2.11 is a sample student information form to be completed by parents and used by the assistance team in formulating a plan to address the concern.)

Responding to Individual Differences in Education, PROJECT R.I.D.E. (1988), is an example of a pupil assistance program that was developed by Great Falls Public Schools under the direction of Dr. Ray Beck and Suellen Gabriel in response to several general and special education needs.

"The overall goal of Project R.I.D.E. is to accommodate the needs of atypical learners in a manner which is as close to the regular classroom as possible. R.I.D.E. provides:

- pre-screening before special education referral,
- a mainstreaming option for those returning from special programs,
- resources for resolving general classroom problems, behavioral and academic, and
- a process for accommodating the special child who does not qualify for pull-out programs.

This program adheres to the theme that every student, whether typical or atypical, belongs to the educational family and should be considered the responsibility of the entire building staff." (RIDE Manual, 1988, p. 3)

Project R.I.D.E. provides guidelines for Schoolwide Assistance Teams, including assessment and record-keeping forms, as well as a menu of effective classroom practices on computer disk and video. For further information regarding this program contact:

PROJECT R.I.D.E.
Sopris West, Inc.
P.O. Box 1809
Longmont, Colorado 80502-1809

MEETING STUDENT NEEDS: ORGANIZATIONAL CHANGE

Current restructuring and reform movements have caused educators to reexamine the organizational structure of schools in terms of meeting individual student needs. Multiage classrooms, learning communities, interdisciplinary teaming, alternative high school scheduling, and magnet schools are some of the terms used to describe ways in which schools and school districts are attempting to restructure the organization of curriculum, facility use, and scheduling to better meet the needs of students.

When considering programs that fundamentally change the schedule, facility use, or staff assignments, it is critical that the administrator understand the dynamics of such a system change. Restructuring to accommodate multiage classrooms, alternative scheduling, learning communities, or interdisciplinary teaming requires thorough and careful planning on the part of the administrator. In order for the program to be successful, there must be buy-in from school personnel. Many of the programs described in this chapter are based on restructuring traditional schedules and organizational structures. If recommendations for restructuring come as a result of school personnel interacting and determining a need for change, the likelihood of significant resistance will be greatly diminished.

A good example of how one school successfully implemented organizational changes that impacted all staff members occurred at Ruth Fyfe Elementary School in Las Vegas, Nevada. During spring planning for the following year the School Site Planning Team disaggregated data collected from staff, parents, and students identifying strengths and weaknesses in the instructional program. The data collected indicated that one of the programs implemented by some teachers that had met with success was cross-age interactions that had occurred as a result of upper grade classes working with younger classes. The school was organized in traditional grade level settings with all students of one age housed in close proximity. For upper grade students to work with a younger class it meant one or the other of the classes had to move across campus. After much discussion it was determined that in order to facilitate and encourage cross age interaction the facility could be used differently, housing mixed grade levels in close proximity. Ruth Fyfe was a well established community school with the average staff tenure being ten to fifteen years. Many members of the staff had been in the same classroom for that same amount of time. Implementing Learning Communities with mixed grade levels would mean at least seventy-five percent of the staff would change classrooms. Had the proposal for change come from the central office or from the administrator it would never have happened without major conflict, but because the recommendation came directly from the staff and was based on data gathered at the school, the concept of Learning Communities was implemented successfully. A great deal of time was spent in dialogue sessions and conversation groups discussing the why and how of such a change.

In this section several programs will be described that are directly related to meeting needs of students, many of which require some organizational restructuring. Some are conceptual models that have been around for awhile but vary in how they are implemented across the country. Administrators must assume the responsibility for exposing the staff and community to innovations or restructuring models that have merit, but they also have the responsibility for making sure such changes occur only as a result of careful planning and research.

Multiage Classrooms

Classrooms that include children of different ages have been created in many schools in an attempt to both address the developmental needs of students and create a real-life learning environment where students have the opportunity to work with students of different ages. Students do not always develop and learn according to legislative time clocks and, because of each child's unique developmental pattern, the traditional grade level configuration has created problems for many children.

Multiage classrooms are not new to the American educational system. Historically such classrooms existed because of enrollment and facility constraints. The one-room school house evokes visions of older students assisting with the education of younger children and a school marm coordinating the learning of all. Philosophical or theoretical beliefs about child development had nothing to do with organizing early multiage classrooms.

Cognitive psychologist Jean Piaget, as mentioned in Chapter 1, proposed that children progress through a series of developmental stages as they construct knowledge about the world, and that children progress through these stages at different rates and at different ages. Piaget's theories about child development have had a powerful impact on educators who acknowledge that the configuration of grade levels frequently does not address the developmental needs of students.

Whitney Elementary School in Las Vegas, Nevada, under the direction of Dr. Francine Mayfield, implemented IMAGE (Integrated Multiage Grouped Education) as a means of recognizing and accommodating student diversity. Multiage classrooms exist both at the primary and intermediate levels, with three grade levels represented in classes. The intent is that students remain in the same class, with the same teacher for three years. While transiency and turnover impact the configuration of some classrooms, there is usually a core that remains intact so that the integrity of the program is maintained.

A brochure developed by the staff at Whitney Elementary states that multiage grouping:

- maximizes a safe and nurturing environment, promoting the physical, social, emotional, and cognitive development of young children
- helps students take responsibility for their behavior and learning
- is based on flexible grouping of children to accommodate their unique timetables for learning
- helps build self-confidence in young children
- fosters positive peer relationships
- de-emphasizes age and competitiveness
- provides a real-life learning environment

- encourages children to respect one another's individuality
- allows children to participate at their own level of learning and social interaction
- is built on continuous student progress
- is child-centered, unlocks graded curriculum boundaries, enhances opportunities for acceleration
- provides peer tutoring opportunities expanding the learning experience for all children
- emphasizes that children develop at different rates and learn in different ways
- enables children to work at a variety of developmental levels without obvious remediation
- reduces the need for grade level retention

For further information regarding IMAGE or Multiage grouping you may contact:

Whitney Elementary School
5005 Kennan Ave.
Las Vegas, Nevada 89105
702-799-7790

LEARNING COMMUNITIES

The most common organizational structure of schools across the country is the self-contained classroom with students assigned to a class based on their chronological age. While the concept of grade levels provides for an efficient means of organizing group of students, it does not take into account the natural real-life learning environment where individuals have the opportunity to interact with and learn from persons of all age groups.

Most educators readily agree that the home and family have a significant impact on the education of a child. In this initial educational setting children are surrounded by individuals of different ages who work together to create and maintain a living environment. Students enter school and for the next twelve years primarily work and play with individual of the same age. Following formal education, high school and possibly college, students enter the world of work and once again are placed in a setting that necessitates interacting and working with individuals of different ages. Many educators are beginning to look at the organizational structure of schools to determine if, in fact, the grade level structure adequately prepares students to enter the world of work, where they will be required to interact with individuals of all different ages.

Several schools in the Clark County School District in Las Vegas, Nevada, have implemented the concept of Learning Communities, which is an organizational structure designed to provide students the opportunity to work with students of different ages and grade levels. This concept is different from Multiage classrooms, which was described earlier. Learning Communities are developed within the school by organizing the use of the school facility to accommodate different age groups working closely together. In other words, different grade level classes are housed in close proximity so that cross-age instructional opportunities may occur. For example, a first grade, second grade, third grade, and fourth grade would be housed in the same hall or wing rather than all the same grade levels being housed together. Most schools that are organized according to this concept house four to five Learning Communities within the school facility.

Katz-McMillan Cooperating Schools in Las Vegas, Nevada, has been organized by Learning Communities for five years. Katz-McMillan is a K through 5, year-round school, with an enrollment of 1,600 students. General guidelines related to the organization of Learning Communities within the school include:

1. more than two grade levels must be represented
2. learning communities should have no less than three and no more than five classrooms
3. special education programs should be included in a learning community

4. inexperienced or new staff must be integrated with experienced staff
5. classrooms within a learning community must be located in close physical proximity

Schools that have implemented the concept of Learning Communities have reported positive outcomes such as:

- increased cross-age interaction
- greater accessibility to various levels of instructional materials
- greater feeling of *our* kids, not *yours* and *mine*
- increased flexibility in meeting individual needs of students
- sense of belonging to a family of learners even amid a large student population
- a buddy system among older and younger students
- increased teacher awareness of curriculum content above and below grade level
- students having the opportunity to interact with more than one teacher
- team approach to handling discipline and academic concerns
- development of team spirit and pride in a noncompetitive atmosphere
- students exposed to different teaching styles
- sharing of resources
- greater sense of accountability for the success of all students
- teachers working as partners to understand the unique characteristics of each grade level

Most schools have not been built to facilitate the concept of Learning Communities and have to make do with the existing facility. In 1993, William R. Lummis Elementary School, Las Vegas, Nevada, was designed and built specifically to accommodate the concept of Learning Communities (Figure 2.4). This architectural design allows for five learning communities, each housing four classrooms opening onto a commons area. Also included in each community is a storage area and an open covered patio leading to the playground. For further information regarding Learning Communities, you may contact:

Katz-McMillan Cooperating Schools
1800 Rock Springs Drive
Las Vegas, Nevada 89128
702-799-4330

Lummis Elementary School
9000 Hillpointe Road
Las Vegas, Nevada 89128
702-799-4380

FIGURE 2.4 WILLIAM R. LUMMIS ELEMENTARY SCHOOL

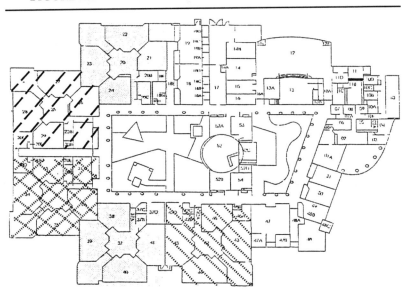

WILLIAM R. LUMMIS ELEMENTARY SCHOOL

INTERDISCIPLINARY MIDDLE SCHOOL TEAMING

Junior high schools, as a means to help adolescence transition between elementary school and high school, changed the configuration of secondary education almost eighty years ago. This organizational change was an attempt to address the unique needs of the young adolescent, recognizing that with the onset of puberty, the way a student thinks and behaves is greatly affected.

In the late 1980s and early 1990s many school districts further altered the organizational structure, moving from the junior high school configuration, grades 7 through 9, to a middle school configuration, grades 6 through 8. Reasons for the change were much the same as those that brought about the organization of junior high schools. A report produced by the Carnegie Council on Adolescent Development, the Task Force on Education of Young Adolescents, entitled Turning Points: Preparing American Youth for the 21st Century (1989), describes the middle grade schools as "potentially society's most powerful force to recapture millions of youth adrift and help every young person thrive . . . ." This report did not just recommend the restructuring of the grade levels included in middle schools but also recommended major transformations in the overall instructional program.

A major recommendation of the Carnegie report (1989) was to create small communities for learning. The key elements of these communities are schools-within-schools or houses, with students and teachers grouped together as teams. Within this type of organizational structure, a team of teachers from different subject areas work and plan together to provide instruction for the same group of students. The purpose of this kind of team effort is to promote communication and cooperation among subject matter specialists and assist the student's transition from one class to another or a self-contained structure to a departmental structure. Figure 2.5 depicts this structure.

The goal of middle school teaming is that instruction be personalized and the focus be on students rather than subjects. An informational brochure created by Theron L. Swainston Middle School, Las Vegas, Nevada, indicates student needs are met by:

FIGURE 2.5 INTERDISCIPLINARY TEAMING AT MIDDLE SCHOOLS

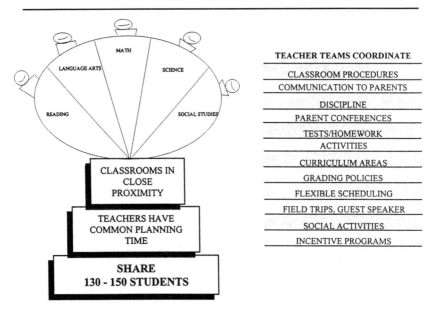

- reducing stress, easing transition to the high school.
- coordinating curriculums among subject areas so that students can relate one subject to another.
- teachers' better understanding of individual differences in students when more than one teacher is making observations and evaluations.
- teachers being more aware of what their students are learning in other classes and what assignments, tests, and projects are making demands on their times.
- common planning leading to more creativity in teaching approaches and consistency in teaching strategies.
- students identifying themselves with a small school within a school, building a sense of belonging.
- parent conferences being arranged for when all academic teachers are available.
- increasing consistency in stating expectations and enforcing rules.

ALTERNATIVE HIGH SCHOOL SCHEDULING

"Current scheduling practices have created a narrow view of human learning, one focusing on recall and recognition, rather than thinking and learning . . . . Learning does not occur by being exposed to knowledge in small non-relational blocks of time . . . ." (Kruse and Kruse, 1995). The Carnegie Standard, which awards credit hours and equates mastery or completion of a subject based on amount of seat time, has served as the backbone for scheduling at secondary schools since the beginning of the twentieth century. Schedules built around the Carnegie Standard often foster instructional methodologies that dispense information in bits and pieces that conform to small blocks of time. In an attempt to address discrepancies in the overall instructional program, many secondary schools have looked at flexible scheduling alternatives.

Changes have been implemented in order to encourage a holistic approach to instruction, increase student learning time, and provide greater amounts of time for laboratory work and student interactive activities. A variety of scheduling labels have emerged that include total block scheduling, varied block scheduling, flexible scheduling, innovative scheduling, and alternative scheduling. While labels are different, each scheduling alternative is an attempt to improve instruction by rearranging the traditional six- to seven-period instructional day.

Scotland County R-1 High School, Memphis, Missouri, in 1990 began researching alternative models of scheduling as reported in the *NASSP Bulletin*, May 1995. After three years of implementation, significant advantages of the eight-block schedule for students attending the Scotland County R-1 High School were identified:

1. Ninety-four-minute periods allow teachers to develop key concepts.
2. Students have a greater range of classes from which to select.
3. Students have two evenings in which to complete class assignments.

4. Students have only four classes to prepare for each day instead of the traditional six or seven.
5. The system allows more creativity on the part of the teacher and fosters the creative abilities of the student.
6. A variety of teaching techniques can be employed in every classroom to reach individual learning styles.
7. A diversity of activities is possible in a ninety-four-minute period, including longer, more complex lab experiments; more in-depth class discussions with fuller participation by all students; field trips; more effective use of films, tapes, or interactive video with time for pre- and postvideo discussions; better opportunities for the teacher to evaluate learning and to give appropriate feedback to students; time for guided homework to begin during the initial meeting of the class; time for staff members to develop quality team-teaching techniques, enhanced instruction for individual students, and more opportunities to foster cooperative learning exercises. (Huff, 1995)

Many high schools across the nation have implemented varying forms of block scheduling, some with a great deal of success, while others have received unfavorable reviews. For further information contact the National Association of Seconday Schools.

MAGNET SCHOOLS

Magnet programs and schools were originally developed as an alternative to forced busing in large urban school districts and have often been implemented as a result of a court order to desegregate, the threat of a court order, or a voluntary decision of the community to establish a magnet program (Joy & Clewell). The establishment of magnet schools was not only a vehicle for voluntary desegregation but also a way to offer students the opportunity to choose educational experiences based on their interests and abilities. Providing students the opportunity to share educational experiences with students from different cultures and backgrounds, who have similar interests and talents, allowed for greater student choice in determining the direction of their education.

It is reported there are more than 5,000 magnet schools across the United States including elementary, middle, and high school age groups. Magnet schools frequently service students that live in a particular neighborhood but also draw from other attendance areas. Magnet schools offer unique, in-depth instructional programs related to a particular theme, in addition to the regular core curriculum. There are a wide variety of magnet school themes that include such offerings as communications, technology, math, science, international studies, intensive foreign language study, and performing arts.

The 1989–90 New York State Magnet School Evaluation Study Executive Summary reports:

- Magnet schools result in reduced racial isolation in schools and assist districtwide desegregation efforts.
- Magnets provide students with added opportunities for integrated learning.
- Magnet schools help to narrow the achievement gap between high- and low-performing students.
- Students in magnet schools are twice as likely to remain in school (not drop out) than students in nonmagnet schools.
- Magnet school students tend to have higher standardized test scores, better attendance rates, and participate in more extracurricular activities.
- Magnet schools benefit students regardless of their race and sex. (Musumeci & Szczypkowski, 1993)
- Magnet schools have been an alternative many school districts have used to address individual differences in student learning, interests, and ability.

SUMMARY

Schools are implementing a variety of guidance programs in an effort to identify and address the individual needs of students. Mediator and tutoring programs are developed primarily to assist students with social, behavioral, or academic problems. Schoolwide teacher assistance teams provide schools with a means of assisting teachers in identifying students with special needs and providing for appropriate interventions.

Organizational restructuring such as multiage classrooms, learning communities, interdisciplinary teaming at middle schools, alternative scheduling, and the identification of magnet schools are attempts by schools and school districts to provide an educational program that will address the unique needs of students and prepare them to be productive citizens in today's society.

Follow-Up Activities

1. Create three role-play situations related to student conflicts that typically occur on the playground or in the lunchroom that could be used in training peer mediators.
2. Brainstorm different things that adult mentors might do to establish and build a relationship with their assigned student. At the elementary level. At the secondary level.
3. Interview a school administrator about the following:

    * special education referral procedures

    * retention procedures and policies

    * student assistance team

    What suggestions might you make to the principal in light of the information shared in this chapter related to the use of schoolwide student assistance teams?
4. Write an article for the PTA newsletter explaining the rationale for creating multiage classrooms for the coming school year.
5. Look at Figure 2.5 (page 38) and under the section Teacher Teams Coordinate select three areas and identify ways the interdisciplinary team might coordinate their efforts.

Resources

Adult Mentor Program
Ms. Janice Connor
2180 Picture Rock Ave.
Henderson, Nevada 89012
(702) 260-3993

Ms. Rosemary Morice
Dallas Public Schools
3700 Ross Ave.
Box 40
Dallas, Texas 75204
(214) 989-8328

Elementary Peer Mediators
Dr. Peggy Moore
James I. Gibson Elementary School
271 Leisure Circle
Henderson, Nevada 89014
(702) 799-8730

Learning Communities
Dr. Dode Worsham and Mrs. Mary Ann Ward
Katz-McMillan Cooperating Schools
1800 Rock Springs Drive
Las Vegas, Nevada 891128
(702) 799-4330

Mr. Rick Watson
Lummis Elementary School
9000 Hillpointe Rd.
Las Vegas, Nevada 89128
(702) 799-4380

Middle Schools
Turning Points: Preparing American Youth for the 21st Century
Carnegie Council on Adolescent Development
P.O. Box 753
Waldorf, Maryland 20694

Multiage Classrooms (IMAGE)
Dr. Francine Mayfield
Whitney Elementary School
5005 Kennan Ave.
Las Vegas, Nevada 89105
(702) 799-7790

School Wide Student Assistance Program
Project R.I.D.E.
Sopris West, Inc.
P.O. Box 1809
Longmont, CO 80502-1809

Secondary-Elementary Tutorial Program
Ms. Donna Barber
c/o A Barber-Cartwright Production
1121 Passion Flower Circle
Las Vegas, Nevada 89108
(702) 647-2746

Secondary Peer Mediation Programs
Peervention: Training Peer Facilitators for Prevention Education
Authors: Robert D. Myrick, Ph.D., and Betsy E. Folk, Ph.D.
Educational Media Corporation
Box 21311
Minneapolis, Minnesota 55421-0311

DOCUMENT 2.1 MENTOR PROGRAM, PROCEDURES

1. Initial contact
   A campus monitor will escort the student to your classroom for the introduction. You will receive a notification prior to the introduction meeting.

2. Establish with the student a time for the weekly meeting.

3. Discuss your role as a mentor.

4. Establish some basic expectations.

5. Discuss general information.
   Class schedule and teachers
   Participation in school activities/clubs/sports
   Family information
   Community activities

6. Discuss the student's concerns/problems.

7. Establish goal(s).
   Short range (for the week or per class)
   Long range (for semester; relationships)

8. Discuss rewards for accomplishments.

9. Monitor progress.
   Weekly conferences
   Check with teachers
   Contact with parents (telephone, Gator-Gram)

10. Maintain a log sheet of conferences/activities/achievements.

Document 2.2 Mentor Program, Guidelines

I. RESPONSIBILITIES
   A. Explain expectations.
      1. Class log
      2. Attendance at weekly conference
      3. Goal sheet
      4. Progress reports
   B. Establish goals.
      1. Assist the student in developing goals
      2. Praise accomplishments
      3. Adjust goals/restate goals not met

> **S** PECIFIC
> **M** EASUREABLE
> **A** TTAINABLE
> **R** EWARDING
> **T** IMEFRAME

II. CONFIDENTIALITY
   A. Establish and assure the student of confidentiality regarding information that is shared with you. Inform the student that you are bound by law to report certain occurrences.
   B. Caution. The discussion of the student's behavior, academics, and goals with teachers is a necessity, but to share the information that the student has confided in you is not appropriate.

III. CREDIBILITY AND TRUST
   A. Keep your promises.
   B. Listen and look for positive characteristics.
   C. Assist the student in developing positive self-esteem attitudes.

IV. REFERRAL
   A. If the student is not making progress and is not attending weekly conferences, inform the dean. Do not discipline.

STUDENTS NEED MORE THAN MONITORS. THEY NEED POSITIVE ROLE MODELS WHO DEMONSTRATE GENUINE CONCERN.

Utilizing Staff and Community 47

Document 2.3 Mentor Program Questionnaire

MENTOR NAME: _____ DATE: _____

SEMESTER 1 2   ADM.   TEACHER   COUNSELOR   SUPPORT

STUDENT INFORMATION:

NAME: _____ GRADE: _____ AGE: _____

SEX: M F

Please check appropriate answers.

1. STUDENT CONTACT
   _____ a. weekly
   _____ b. more than once a week
   _____ c. at least four times during the semester
   _____ d. other _____

2. PARENT CONTACT
   _____ a. phone call
   _____ b. personal conference
   _____ c. at least four times during the semester
   _____ d. other _____

3. METHODS USED WITH MY STUDENT INCLUDED
   _____ informal talks/listening
   _____ rewards
   _____ notes to parents
   _____ reviewing progress reports
   _____ setting goals
   _____ introducing to other peers
   _____ enlisting in a school club
   _____ enlisting in a sport
   _____ academic tutoring
   _____ checking homework
   _____ help develop a time management schedule
   _____ reviewing a log kept by student
   _____ sending special notes (birthday card)
   _____ sharing a meal

List other methods that you used to assist your student

_____

_____

DOCUMENT 2.4 MENTOR PROGRAM
STUDENT PROGRESS

RATE THE STUDENT'S PROGRESS/IMPROVEMENT ON A SCALE OF ONE THROUGH FIVE.

	NONE	POOR	AVERAGE	GOOD	EXCELLENT
A. ATTENDANCE	1	2	3	4	5
B. BEHAVIOR	1	2	3	4	5
C. ACADEMICS	1	2	3	4	5
D. ATTITUDE	1	2	3	4	5
E. GOALS	1	2	3	4	5
F. RELATIONSHIPS WITH PEERS	1	2	3	4	5
WITH TEACHERS	1	2	3	4	5
WITH FAMILY	1	2	3	4	5

COMMENTS/SUGGESTIONS FOR IMPROVEMENTS IN THE PROGRAM:

_____

_____

_____

List problems that you encountered: _____

_____

_____

_____

Document 2.5 Mentor Program Contact/Conference Log

MENTOR: _____

STUDENT: _____ GRADE: _____

DATE ASSIGNED: _____

DATE	CONTACT/CONFERENCE LOG

Document 2.6 Parent Letter

Date:

TO THE PARENT OR GUARDIAN OF:

Student No:

One of the goals of _____ High School is to see that all students have educational success. The Mentor Program is designed to serve students who would benefit from a one-on-one caring support system within the school. Your child has been recommended for the mentor program.

Each student in this program is assigned to a staff mentor. The staff person acts as a mentor to the student throughout the semester. The student is required to complete a daily log and to check in with his/her mentor at regularly scheduled times. The mentor is responsible for the following areas: 1. monitoring the student's academic progress, 2. advising the student in setting goals, and 3. giving the student encouragement and challenges.

Your child was interviewed, assigned a mentor, and has agreed to be in the mentor program. If you do not want your child to be a part of this program, please call the school. If you want additional information about the Mentor Program, please contact the school.

Your child's staff mentor is _____.

Sincerely yours,

DOCUMENT 2.7 SCHOOLWIDE STUDENT ASSISTANCE TEAM, REQUEST FOR ASSISTANCE

Name of Child:_____Date:_____
Birthdate:_____Grade:_____Teacher:_____

SCHOOL RECORDS REVIEW

Health _____
Special Programs _____
Retention _____
Attendance _____
Transiency _____
Behavior (Detentions/Suspensions) _____
Other_____

AREA(S) OF CONCERN

Briefly describe what you would like the student to be able to do that he/she does not presently do.

Behavioral:_____
_____

Academic:_____
_____

Identify Areas of Strength:_____
_____

PRIOR INTERVENTIONS

Schoolwide Programs:_____
_____

Classroom Interventions:_____
_____

Outside of School:_____

Document 2.8 Student Assistance Plan of Action

STUDENT NAME:

INTERVENTION METHODS/STRATEGIES: (Include type of strategy, resources needed, personnel, and timeline.)

OUTCOME OF INTERVENTION:

FURTHER RECOMMENDATION(S):

_____ Continue current strategy
_____ Try another strategy
_____ Assistance is no longer needed
_____ Proceed with referral procedure for:
    _____ Counseling
    _____ Special Education Testing
    _____ ESL
    _____ Speech
    _____ Other _____

DOCUMENT 2.9 TRACKING FORM

Date of Initial Request _____

Name of Student _____ Grade ____
Teacher _____
Team member assigned to monitor case: _____

Date of initial meeting with teacher: _____

- ☐ Review and clarify request for assistance
- ☐ Determine additional data needed
- ☐ Determine a plan of action
- ☐ Schedule followup meeting

NOTES

TO BE COMPLETED BY NEXT MEETING	
TASK:	ASSIGNED TO:

Date of followup meeting: _____

Document 2.10 Letter to Parents

Date

Dear Parents,

Your child,_____, is experiencing some academic and/or behavioral difficulties at school. As his/her teacher I am concerned and realize there are many different reasons why a student might be having such difficulties. As a result, I am planning to conduct some informal assessments related to the area(s) of concern in order to determine an appropriate course of action. I will be reviewing your child's previous school records and consulting with other teachers and school staff to devise a plan to address these concerns.

Enclosed you will find a Student Information Form. Please complete this form and return it to me as soon as possible. This form provides background information that may be helpful in understanding your child's difficulties.

Following this data gathering period I will contact you so that we can discuss the results and what we should do next to help resolve these concerns.

If you have any questions regarding these assessments please feel free to contact me at_____. The best time to reach me is_____.

Sincerely,

Teacher

IMPORTANT NOTICE

In rare instance learning and/or behavioral difficulties can be the result of an educational handicap, including emotion disorders and specific learning disabilities.

At this time, we have <u>NO</u> reason to believe that your child is handicapped or even potentially handicapped. However, should this assessment identify your child as <u>potentially</u> handicapped, you will be immediately notified and requested to give your written consent for a formal special education evaluation of your child. You will also be informed of your parental rights and the procedural safeguards that will be followed. You may request a copy of these rights and safeguards by contacting the school.

Document 2.11 Student Information Form

Student Name:_____ Date:_____
Birthdate:_____ Age:_____ Sex:_____

Parent Name:_____
Address:_____
Home Phone:_____ Work Phone:_____

HEALTH HISTORY

Medical problems during pregnancy? No____ Yes____
Complications at birth? No____ Yes____
Medical problems as an infant? No____ Yes____
Current medical problems? No____ Yes____
Hearing problems? No____ Yes____
Vision problems? No____ Yes____
Coordination problems? No____ Yes____
Delayed crawling/walking? No____ Yes____
Delayed speaking? No____ Yes____
Any areas that were answered yes please explain: _____
_____
_____

EDUCATIONAL HISTORY

Attended preschool? No____ Yes____
Attended kindergarten? No____ Yes____
Ever retained? No____ Yes____ What grade?_____
Attended special classes? No____ Yes____ If yes, explain: _____

Describe any learning or school problems:_____
_____

Describe study habits at home: _____
_____

Indicate number of schools students has attended:_____

3

STUDENT GUIDANCE: DEVELOPING STUDENT SOCIAL RESPONSIBILITY

In Chapter 2, the focus was on meeting social and academic needs of students using resources at the school level (schoolwide assistance teams) and using the facility (learning communities, magnet schools, etc.) in a variety of innovative ways. In order to put the primary focus on instruction, there needs to be an atmosphere at the school that promotes learning. Referring back to Miguel in Chapter 1, imagine the amount of learning that is disrupted when he causes a major stir in the classroom. How do we maintain a positive environment in which students begin to take responsibility for themselves? How do we deal with those severe behavior problems that appear to be more and more a part of the normal school day? This chapter takes a look at successful incentive programs and schoolwide discipline plans that promote social and academic growth.

STUDENT INCENTIVE PROGRAMS

As mentioned in the first chapter, most students from the age of six to twelve view themselves as capable and valuable individuals in a school. This knowledge should help us as administrators to set up incentives or recognition programs based on the social development of children that encourage students to do their best or to recognize individuals. Incentive programs can be developed and implemented by the administrator, staff, or parents. Involving more members of the staff ensures greater success and buy-in by all. Incentive programs can range from simple activities such as Story N' Snack (described below) to more elaborate programs such as Smart Cards or monthly assemblies. The following pages list different incentives that have been successful for K through 12 students with samples of forms, letters, and notes that announce or promote these activities. As administrators, we have successfully used the elementary samples.

ELEMENTARY INCENTIVES

Story N' Snack. Held once a week, two to three students from each classroom are invited to join the administrator or another staff member in the front lobby or central area to hear a story. The criteria for selection are left up to the teachers, with the goal being that all children eventually have a chance to participate. Following the reading of a story, each student receives a snack or small treat. This easy incentive is also an extremely valuable experience for administrators. Administrators have found this to be an important way to communicate and just talk to children. Parents see this as a positive administrator-student interaction.

Monthly Luncheons with Administrators. Students who have demonstrated excellent behavior, completed all assignments, or improved significantly in one or more areas are invited to have lunch with the administrator. Lunch can be provided by the school or students can bring their own. Invitations are given to each teacher who then selects one student to attend. This usually occurs fifteen to thirty minutes before the regular lunch schedule providing additional time for meaningful dialogue among students and the principal. Several schools have set up partnerships with local fast-food chains who provide some or all of the lunch as part of a community effort. Sometimes just providing dessert makes this a special time for children.

Newcomer's Luncheon with Administrators. With a transient population, we found it beneficial to invite new students to a luncheon. This helps students feel more comfortable in their new surroundings and gives them an opportunity to meet other new students and staff members. This also gives principals an opportunity to meet new students and make them more aware of school procedures. We know of one school that also invites the parents to join them for lunch on that day. Invitations are given out ahead of time, which allows communication with parents and teachers.

Newcomer's Coupon Book. These booklets are given to each student who enrolls after the first of the school year. Students may use each coupon at any time with their teacher's approval. Ideas range from a pencil from the office manager to fifteen minutes with the administrator. Elementary students and parents have stated that these coupons are very valuable in helping new students feel like part of the school. See Figure 3.1.

Pat on the Back. Sometimes students deserve a special pat on the back because they have made great progress, turned in their homework, or have not been tardy for a period of time. This special Principal's Award is given to students when teachers notify the administrator using the short form pictured on page 61. The easy-to-fill-out form is used by the administrator to recognize that individual or a group of individuals. We have given Pats on the Back for reading groups, students who have published or written a story, and for those who made it through lunch recess without a single referral for a whole week. By changing the reward (certificate, phone call home, sticker, etc.) students eagerly wait to be called to the office. See Figure 3.2.

Postcard Home. Sometimes the most rewarding thing that a principal can do is to send home a little note of praise. Every few months, we ask teachers to give us a list of four or five students who could benefit from a positive note home. Each teacher is asked to write a brief description of why this student is being recommended, which is then conveyed to the parents through a postcard in the mail. See Figure 3.3.

FIGURE 3.1 NEWCOMER'S COUPON BOOK

Bring this coupon to our 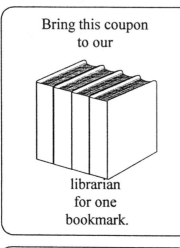 librarian for one bookmark.

This coupon entitles you to one free juice from our lunchroom.

Bring this coupon to the clerk for one HUG!

Bring this coupon to the student store for one free treat.

Developing Student Social Responsibility

Figure 3.2 Pat on the Back

PRINCIPAL'S AWARD: Teacher's Name _____   Track ____   Grade ____

Student(s) names to be awarded:

_____
_____
_____
_____

Reason for Pat on the Back:

_____
_____
_____
_____

WELL DONE

Action taken by Principal:

____ Certificate   ____ Treat from Goodie Jar
____ Phone Call Home   ____ Sticker
____ Other

FIGURE 3.3 POSTCARD HOME

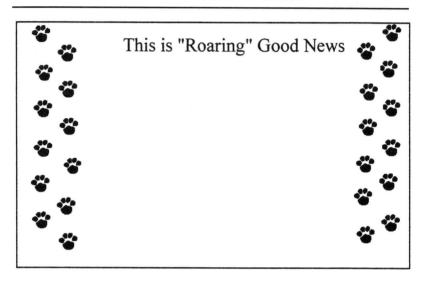

Birthday Cards. A birthday card is sent to each child from the school during the month of his/her birthday. Often students will stop and let the office know that they received their card and how special it made them feel. A school birthday card may be designed and mailed home by office staff at the beginning of each month for all birthdays during the month.

Birthday Books. A highly successful incentive program involves presenting each child with a paperback book during the month of his/her birthday. This idea helps promote the love of reading, while building a child's own library. Books are ordered through book clubs or fairs with the cost being defrayed by grants, fund raiser, and/or parent-teacher associations. All books are stamped: Happy Birthday from _____ Elementary School.

Student/Citizen of the Month. Many elementary schools have monthly assemblies to honor the student of the month. Teachers are asked to select one student from their class based on guidelines dealing with academics or citizenship. Parents are often invited to the assembly and receive a certificate or note honoring their child. Bumper stickers are also given to parents that read: My child was a student/citizen of the month at _____ School.

Student of the Week. Classroom teachers often set up a Student of the Week program where one particular child is highlighted for that week. Children are encouraged to bring pictures and favorite articles from home. They are given extra privileges for that week. Teachers have found this to be beneficial as it gives children a special time of their own and helps the class learn more about the uniqueness of each person.

Most elementary schools have developed incentive programs that reflect the name of the school, the name of the school's mascot, or have incorporated commercial ideas such as "Catch 'em Being Good." Some of the schools provide staff with tickets to pass out to students who are demonstrating appropriate behavior. When students collect a certain number of tickets they turn them in for a reward or prize. Incentive programs that are easy to implement, consistent, and involve the entire school appear to have the most success.

Local businesses have set up partnerships with school districts. In particular, Pizza Hut, TCBY, Sizzler, and TGIF offer free meals to students for outstanding success in school. Teachers are responsible for recognizing individual students, filling in the forms, and having the principal sign the forms. As mentioned previously, local fast-food chains are often willing to provide monthly luncheons, drinks, or fries as part of their community effort.

MIDDLE SCHOOL/JUNIOR HIGH/HIGH SCHOOL INCENTIVES

Students of the Month. Students of the Month, in most secondary schools, are selected by each department (art, business, English, etc.) for outstanding work. These students usually receive a certificate, and their pictures are featured on the Student of the Month display board. Their pictures are also displayed in the monthly newsletter sent to all families. In addition, many secondary schools have partnered with local restaurants or other businesses to honor these students at a luncheon or to provide prizes and awards.

Athlete of the Month. This recognition is similar to Student of the Month except that it is designated by the athletic department for each team or individual sport sponsored by that school. A certificate is awarded to each student along with his or her picture being displayed on the Athlete of the Month display. Letters are sent home to family members with other prizes being given, such as a school T-shirt, coupons from community businesses, etc.

Honor Rolls (SMART Cards). Students are recognized in the monthly newsletter at grading time for Straight A Honor Roll and for A and B Honor Roll. Many of the secondary schools in the Clark County School District, Las Vegas, Nevada, have partnered with community services to provide coupons to honor roll students offering discounts or gift items. The SMART Card (Student and Merchant Achievement Recognition Team) is issued to eligible students (those who achieve a 3.0 GPA or better) entitling students to a 15 percent discount on goods purchased from participating merchants. This card recognizes students for their outstanding academic achievement.

At the secondary level, other honors are given to students through organizations such as National Honor Society, Rotary Clubs, and group honors (chorus, music departments, etc.). Many local and national businesses (Pizza Hut, McDonald's, TCBY, etc.) offer certificates, free meals, or other products to students for outstanding achievement. These coupons and certificates are provided for teachers to use as incentives for their students. Because adolescents do not want to be perceived as different or to be singled out, many high schools selectively set up recognition awards to benefit all students.

SCHOOLWIDE DISCIPLINE PROGRAMS

One of educators' main goals is to help students become responsible for their learning and behavior. With the trend toward site-based management, schools are writing mission statements that involve staff, parents, and students. Improvement targets are developed from data collected and emphasize meeting the instructional and social needs of students. An integral part of any school is the atmosphere that prevails through an effective discipline program or plan. If the goal is to have all students motivated to learn, providing a safe environment conducive to learning is essential.

When designing a schoolwide discipline program, it is necessary to keep two things in mind. One is the stages of human growth and development as outlined in Chapter 1, and the other is the need to involve all staff in the planning and implementation stages. Knowing how students perceive their surroundings and authority figures is vital in planning. Setting up rules and consequences will vary according to the age group of the students at the school. Surveying staff members to gather data before executing a schoolwide discipline program will show areas of needed improvement or concerns that must be dealt with in planning and implementing a discipline program. The more the staff and parents are involved, the more effective a program will be.

Many school districts have district guidelines, policies and regulations, absenteeism/attendance policies, and may prescribe appropriate consequences for delinquent behavior. These, then, must be communicated to staff, students, and parents. The most widely accepted means of communication to parents is through a parent newsletter or a parent brochure that outlines the steps involved. Basically, a schoolwide discipline program or plan starts with communicating the school's philosophy and/or expectations. These expectations can be as simple as: Be kind and work hard, or they may be more elaborate such as:

- No student will interfere with teacher instruction.
- No student will interfere with another student's learning.
- No student will engage in any behavior that is not in his/her best interest or in the best interest of others.

After the expectations are set, then schoolwide rules are listed, including district policies, along with consequences. At the elementary level, rules are usually listed in a positive manner and address dress codes, behavior in the lunchroom and playground, and behavior in the classroom. At the secondary level, rules may include appropriate behavior on or off campus, dress codes, and identify specific consequences such as immediate referrals to the dean or assistant principal, expulsion, required parent conferences, and suspensions. Student handbooks explaining rules and consequences are developed and issued to each student at the beginning of the school year. Effective schoolwide discipline plans may also include the responsibilities of the administrator, teacher, and parent as well as the student.

In addition to the expectations, rules, and consequences, most schools at both the elementary and secondary level develop a student discipline referral form where teachers can report major problems, channeling them to the proper authority.

These referral plans are based on the needs of each individual school according to organizational management and available assistance. Documents 3.1 to 3.10, at the end of this chapter, are actual discipline plans, letters to parents and students, and referral forms that have been successful at elementary and secondary schools. These may be altered to fit the needs of a school or may be used as written.

Rules, consequences, and a referral system are all key components to an effective discipline plan. However, essential additions to this design are effective and efficient ways to promote student self-responsibility in order to prevent misbehaviors. Students learn responsibility best when they are called upon to be responsible. Responsible students make good decisions based on careful evaluation of different situations. At the school site, providing students with experiences in which they can make choices is a logical step in assisting them in becoming more responsible. Educators generally agree that the most common classroom misbehaviors result when students are trying to gain the teacher's attention, get attention from their peers, or escape from some unpleasant activity. Sometimes misbehavior occurs as a result of boredom, frustration, or fatigue. This is often observed with students who frequently get out of their seats to sharpen pencils, go to the restroom, throw papers away, or misbehave in order to be sent out of the classroom.

Obviously the best solution for these types of misbehaviors is the implementation of effective classroom management techniques and motivating, engaging lessons. Educators who practice proactive interventions are those who have the fewest discipline problems.

When students do not follow the rules and are referred to the principal's office or dean's office, a consequence is usually given. If the offense continues, then a behavior plan may be put in place. A behavior plan, behavior modification contract or agreement, written cooperatively by the teacher, student, and parents, can assist a student in taking control over his/her behavior by providing the opportunity for the student to make better choices. Gene Bedley, in his book *The Big R Responsibility*, states that "change will occur when we increase children's awareness of responsibility and present the benefits for being responsible. Children tend to do whatever works for them. If being irresponsible gets more attention, they will not learn responsibility" (1992, p. 28).

Behavior Contracts. A behavior contract or agreement focuses on the responsibility of the student, the teacher, and parents. Together this group looks at the types of behaviors that are not acceptable and then states the behaviors that are acceptable. There are several steps to include as part of a behavior program, as outlined by Robert Slavin (1994). These are:

1. Identifying one or two behaviors to target first, in order to see what reinforcers maintain the behavior. This requires the teacher to observe the student over a period of time, aiming at addressing one specific area instead of many. In the classroom, the three reinforcers that maintain most misbehaviors are teacher's attention, peer's attention, and release from boredom, fatigue, and frustration.

2. Establishing a baseline behavior by observing the student over a period of time to see how often the behavior occurs. Baseline measurements may include frequency (how many times it occurs) and/or the amount of time (how many minutes it occurs).

3. Selecting incentives and criteria that reinforce appropriate behavior. These reinforcers may be reduced over time and typically include praise, privileges, and tangible rewards.

4. Selecting consequences and criteria for consequences as necessary. This may need to be utilized when a serious behavior problem does not respond to a reinforcement or incentive program. There is a difference between consequences and punishments. Punishment is a form of retribution—basically, the violator pays for the misbehavior. Fear is the primary motivator. Consequences, on the other hand, are related to the rule and are logical, natural, and viewed as instructional rather than punitive. When select-

ing consequences, the rule of thumb is to use them sparingly, know the difference between consequences and punishments, make sure the student understands the reasons for the consequence, provide ways for the student to obtain positive reinforcement, and avoid physical consequences.

5. Observing and comparing behavior to the baseline. Each behavior plan needs to be assessed for its effectiveness. A behavior plan should show improvement within a few days; if not, a revision of different reinforcers may be needed.

6. Reducing the frequency of reinforcement (incentives). As the student's behavior begins to improve, the frequency of the reinforcement may be reduced or stretched out. Reducing the frequency helps maintain the appropriate behavior over the long run.

For elementary students, the behavior contract is short, working on one or two behaviors with appropriate incentives and/or consequences. Secondary behavior contracts are often more involved and detailed with goals and objectives being outlined. Samples of these contracts can be found at the end of this chapter, Documents 3.11 through 3.16. Behavior Modification Plans, Behavior Contracts, or Behavior Agreements are all based on principles of behavioral learning theories. Some educators object to behavior modification strategies on the premise that students are being rewared for doing what they are suppose to be doing. It is important to keep in mind that all classrooms in some way use rewards and consequences (such as praise, grades, suspensions, etc.). Behavior modification strategies provide a more systematic way to use the rewards while keeping consequences to a minimum. It should be noted that individual behavior modification plans should be implemented when effective classroom management techniques are not enough to maintain an atmosphere for learning.

Other interventions at the classroom level include providing a time-out area where students can consider their behavior, reflect on the problem, and think about how they might have handled the situation differently. A poster or worksheet is attached to the area with statements to be completed by the student (see Figure 3.4).

FIGURE 3.4 TIME TO THINK

I am having trouble with _____

Where _____

When _____

What happened _____

What I did about it _____

How I might have handled it differently _____

This type of intervention allows the student to examine his/her behavior and to see how the situation might be solved differently. Role-playing situations and watching films or videos pertaining to how to deal with inappropriate behavior are all proactive ways that help students become responsible for their actions.

Serious Behavior Problems. What about students who demonstrate serious behavior problems? What about the Miguels? As previously stated, schools play an important role in preventing serious misbehavior and providing a safe environment for all students. According to Slavin's research (1994), there are seven guidelines for prevention of delinquency and serious misbehavior. These are:

1. Understanding the causes of misbehavior. It is essential that educators look at each individual student to understand the cause of misbehavior. For some students who are not successful in school, rewards for hard work and good behavior appear small and meaningless; therefore they look for other rewards. Others find acceptance in groups that go against the norms of achievement and good citizenship.
2. Enforcing the rules and practices. Students need to understand that the rules will be enforced. Expectations need to be communicated continually with students seeing misbehavior being corrected.
3. Enforcing school attendance. Research has shown that truancy and delinquency are strongly related. Those who are out of school often are those who are causing problems in the community. Incentives for promoting attendance is a viable option for any school.
4. Accommodating for instruction. Motivational and engaging lessons appropriate to the age group that provide for individualization and group work have been found to reduce discipline problems. Students who have been tracked or grouped according to ability and are considered the low group often show antisocial behavior and are most likely to be unsuccessful in school. This again promotes boredom and frustration and leads to misbehavior.
5. Practicing interventions. As noted previously, classroom management strategies are the key to improving student behavior. Besides individual interventions, use of collaborative groups, especially at the secondary level, have been found to be an effective way to promote appropriate behavior. This goes back to Chapter 1, dealing with human growth stages during adolescence.
6. Requesting family involvement. Parents or legal guardians need to be involved any time serious misbehavior occurs. They should be involved in help-

ing establish a behavior modification plan and also a home plan.
7. Judiciously applying consequences. This last guideline involves the implementation of punishments that should be used only as needed and be appropriate to the offense. Many educators feel that suspension should be used only for the most serious offenders because it often leads to truancy problems as students begins to fall behind in their work.

Other suggestions for punishments are time-out, detention rooms, or loss of privileges. Any punishment given should not last too long, and the student should then be reinstated into the school situation. It is important that a student feel accepted as a member of the class.

Students who continually misbehave or show signs of emotional problems at home or at school should be referred to the school counselor. Descriptions of student guidance and counseling services are outlined in Chapter 4.

ADDITIONAL RESOURCES

There are several commercial products that have been recognized as effective and successful. Lee Canter's Assertive Discipline Plan has been successfully implemented in many schools and districts. As mentioned in Chapter 2, any plan or program needs to fit the philosophy and needs of the particular school, staff, parents, and students. Information regarding Lee Canter's work may be found in the Resources section of this chapter.

A resource that focuses entirely on the identification of and interventions for severe acting-out behaviors is a video series titled *Managing Acting-Out Behavior: A Staff Development Program to Prevent and Manage Acting-Out Behavior*, written by Geoffrey Colvin, Ph.D. This video series provides teachers with observation techniques to identify specific acting-out behaviors and gives strategies for dealing with these behaviors. This video may be used in staff development training with small groups of staff in order to provide time to dialogue and set up procedures. It is helpful to review the video from time to time.

Other resources that may be helpful include student-interactive videos (distributed by Sunburst Videos and listed in the Resources), dealing with specific topics such as:

- Ten Things to Do Instead of Hitting (K–2)
- I Get So Mad (K–2)
- All About Anger (2–4)
- Let's Talk About Responsibility (5–9)
- Anger: You Can Handle It (7–12)

These videos allow for small group discussions while providing interventions and positive ways to deal with everyday situations. Shown in the classroom, these presentations build a classroom atmosphere of trust between students and teachers.

SUMMARY

Incentives, schoolwide discipline plans, and the implementation of effective classroom management techniques are all basic to helping students become responsible citizens. When students have the opportunity to make good decisions, help to design rules and consequences, and know that they are valued, they feel ownership of the school's philosophy and expectations. Educators need to recognize that during different developmental stages students will perceive and respond to different sets of expectations, rules, and consequences. By providing knowledge and training of human developmental stages to staff, a school will have a better understanding of how to meet students' social as well as academic needs.

FOLLOW-UP ACTIVITIES

1. Grade level chairpersons or department heads come to you, as the administrator, with concerns about inconsistency with the existing schoolwide discipline plan. Develop a plan for redesigning and implementing such a plan.

2. Your assistant principal wants to set up some recognition programs to promote self-esteem and student responsibility. Which of the ideas presented would you suggest and how would they be implemented?
3. Referring to Miguel in Chapter 1, what type of behavioral plan would you design? Who would be involved and what consequences would be effective?

Resources

Assertive Discipline for Parents
Lee Canter
Harper & Row, Publishers

Managing Acting-out Behavior: A Staff Development Program to Prevent and Manage Acting-out Behavior
Geoffrey Colvin, Ph.D.
Behavior Associates
P.O. Box 6533
Eugene, Oregon 97405-0633
(541) 485-6450

Sunburst Complete Video Catalog
Grades K - 12
Dept. SG07
101 Castleton Street
P.O. Box 100
Pleasantville, New York 10579-0100
1-800-431-1934

NAESP (National Association of Elementary School Principals)
1615 Duke Sreet
Alexandria, Virginia 22314-33483
1-800-386-2377

Document 3.1 Discipline Plan

Dear Parents:

Because discipline in the schools continues to be of optimum concern nationwide and because principals and teachers have the responsibility for providing an environment in which children can learn, the principals, and other staff members at our school will emphasize a plan that stresses positive self-discipline. The plan includes the following two rules:

1. Be Kind
2. Work Hard

The plan is based on the following assumptions:
1. We have no major disruptive problems at our school
2. Our students are capable of fulfilling our expectations.
3. Parents must and do play a major role in our efforts to make students self-responsible.
4. The entire staff (principal, assistant principal, teachers, secretaries, aides, custodians), with the cooperation of parents, must be and are involved in and consistent in correcting behavior.
5. A superb instructional program must be and is a major part of the plan.
6. All adults must set desirable examples.
7. Positive recognition must be given frequently to deserving students.
8. Consistent and prompt follow-through must be incorporated into the program.
9. Students must be aware of how their behavior affects other, in a positive as well as a negative way.
10. Students must feel valued.
11. Students must learn the importance of working hard.

The following guidelines have been established:
1. Good manners will be practiced by all staff members and students.
2. Parents will be immediately informed by telephone and/or written communication of unacceptable behavior.
3. Recognition will be given to students for their accomplishments.
4. Students will reflect on how their behavior affects others and consider ways to improve unacceptable behavior.
5. Our doors are always open to our parents. Welcome!

Because it is imperative that education be shared responsibility between the home and school, we ask that you carefully review the attached. Keep in mind that our goal is to establish an environment in which teachers can successfully teach and children can comfortably and successfully learn with minimal disruption and maximum joy. Your support is appreciated! Thank you!

DOCUMENT 3.1 DISCIPLINE PLAN, CONTINUED

Instructional Expectations

1. Students will work hard at all times.
2. Students will arrive on time for school with a positive attitude.
3. Students will maintain regular attendance. Excessive absences will be avoided.
4. Students will complete all assigned work. Emphasis should be on quality, accuracy, and neatness.

BEHAVIORAL EXPECTATIONS

1. Students will act in a responsibility and cooperative manner. Fighting will not be tolerated.
2. Students will treat everyone with courtesy and respect. Profane language and/or disrespectful actions will not be used.
3. Students will be kind. No one will make another feel unworthy.
4. Students will respect school property and the property of others.
5. Students will play and use equipment in a safe manner.
6. Students will seek help when a problem occurs.
7. Students will walk and talk in a quiet and orderly manner.
8. Students will dress in accordance with the school district dress code. Inappropriate attire includes: thongs, strapless sandals, tank or bare midriff tops, and clothing that is transparent, low-cut, or strapless. Clothing must be at least fingertip length. Students are not allowed to wear hats on campus unless a designated activity has been planned (such as hat day).
9. Students will keep candy, chewing gum, toys, radios, sports equipment, and valuables at home.

Developing Student Social Responsibility

Document 3.1 Discipline Plan, continued

Steps for Correcting Inappropriate Behavior

A top priority at our school is to have each teacher spend as much time as possible directly involved with the instruction of all students. A good instructional environment is dependent on good school and classroom behavior. Student discipline is an area where the school and the home share joint responsibility. Full understanding and close cooperation between the school and the home will result in a more relaxed and productive atmosphere for all students.

Most students want to, and do, behave properly. When behavior is not acceptable, the school provides guidance and structure necessary to bring about improvement.

The following procedure will be used:

1. If the behavior of a student is determined to be unacceptable, a behavior referral will be issued. This referral can be initiated by any school personnel. The referral is then sent to the office and the appropriate action will be taken by school administration. A copy of the referral and the action taken will be given to parents, the adult issuing the referral, and the classroom teacher. A copy is maintained in the student's behavior file.

2. The school administrator will take one or more of the following actions when a student is referred.

    a. The student will be conferenced by the Principal of Assistant Principal.

    b. Parents will be notified from the Principal's office of the misbehavior by means of the referral or a phone call.

    c. The referral will note disciplinary action to be taken.

    d. A required parent conference will be held before a student may return to school.

    e. Parents will be advised that the student will be suspended for a certain number of days.

    f. A copy of the discipline report and the citations will be retained in the student's discipline file.

DOCUMENT 3.2 STUDENT RULES OF CONDUCT

Instructional Expectations

1. Complete all assigned work emphasizing quality, accuracy, and neatness.

2. Arrive at school on time prepared for instruction.

3. Maintain regular daily attendance.

Behavioral Expectations

1. Act in a responsible and cooperative manner. Fighting will not be tolerated.

2. Treat all student and adults with courtesy and respect. Profane language and/or disrespectful actions will not be tolerated.

3. Be kind and courteous of the feelings of others. Do not tease, degrade, or disgrace another student.

4. Seek help when a problem occurs.

5. Respect and care for school property and the property of others.

6. Play and use school equipment and facilities in a safe manner. Play in assigned playground areas.

7. Dress in accordance with district dress code. Inappropriate attire includes thongs; strapless sandals; hemlines ABOVE midthigh length; tank tops and bare midriff attires; transparent, lowcut or strapless clothing; attire with controversial or obscene slogans/advertisements that disrupt the instructional setting.

8. Walk and talk in a quiet and orderly manner.

9. Keep candy, chewing gum, toys, radios, sports equipment, and valuables at home.

DOCUMENT 3.2 STUDENT RULES OF CONDUCT, CONTINUED

DISCIPLINE PROCEDURES

LEVEL 1   The first occurrence of student misbehavior is discussed between the student and teacher.

LEVEL 2   After the second occurrence, the parent is notified by the teacher in a weekly progress report or phone call and asked to assist with the correction of the problem.

LEVEL 3   The third occurrence results in a conference attended by the teacher, parent, and student.

LEVEL 4   After the fourth occurrence, a required conference is held with the principal, teacher, parent, and student. The student is released from school under the parent's supervision until the conference is held.

(Flagrant misbehavior demonstrated by a student will result in immediate principal-teacher-parent contact as describe in level 4.)

Please help your child become an effective problem solver by reviewing the following steps with him/her:

SOLVE ALL PROBLEMS WITH YOUR HEAD AND YOUR HEART -- NOT YOUR HAND!

1. Think before you act.
2. Talk it over.
3. Walk away.
4. See an adult (teacher, playground monitor, or principal).
5. Be kind. Remember fighting is NOT a solution!

Our staff is committed to teaching and reinforcing appropriate student behavior. Courtesy and respect is practiced by all staff members and students. Students are encouraged to follow school rules of conduct, set a good example for others, and reflect on how their behavior affects others. With your cooperation and help we can provide a positive, productive learning environment for your child.

Document 3.3 Elementary Student Discipline Referral

DATE: _____ TIME: _____

STUDENT: _____ TEACHER: _____

DESCRIPTION OF INCIDENT: _____
_____

ACTION TAKEN BY THE TEACHER PRIOR TO REFERRAL:

    _____ Conference with student   _____ Letter to parent
    _____ Phone call home   _____ Conference with parents

ACTION TAKEN BY THE PRINCIPAL OR ASSISTANT PRINCIPAL:

    _____ Conference with student   _____ Restriction from recess
    _____ Phone call to parents   _____ In-school suspension in office
    _____ Conference with parents required   _____ Conference with parents required due to the seriousness of the incident. This student may not return to school until a conference is held or scheduled. Please call for an appointment.

STUDENT'S ACTION PLAN: _____
_____
_____

PLEASE REMIND YOUR CHILD TO:
    _____ Be kind   _____ Work without bothering others
    _____ Work hard   _____ Get to class on time
    _____ Think before acting   _____ Seek help when faced with a problem
    _____ Respect others   _____ Solve a problem without fighting
    _____ Follow directions
    _____ Use appropriate language
    _____ Show respect for school property

ACTION BY PARENT:
Parents, please discuss the above described issue with your child and remind him/her to be a kind, hardworking students. Describe your plan of action to correct the problem below. Please see that your child returns this tomorrow with your signature. Thank you.

PARENT ACTION PLAN: _____
_____

Home Phone Number _____ Work Phone Number_____
Parent's Signature _____

DOCUMENT 3.4 COMMUNICATION WITH PARENTS, CHARMING BEHAVIOR

CHARMING BEHAVIOR

STUDENT: _____

IT'S A PLEASURE TO TAKE TIME TO COMMUNICATE WITH THE FAMILY OF STUDENTS WHO CONTRIBUTE POSITIVELY TO THE EDUCATIONAL ENVIRONMENT IN OUR CLASSROOM FOR MATHEMATICS.

YOUR STUDENT CONTRIBUTES POSITIVELY:

_____ IS WELL-MANNERED AND COURTEOUS

_____ IS KIND AND CONSIDERATE TO OTHERS

_____ PAYS ATTENTION WHEN INSTRUCTED

_____ WORKS HARD IN CLASS

_____ KEEPS THE WORK AREA NEAT AND CLEAN

_____ TURNS IN NEAT, THOROUGH WORK

_____ IS PUNCTUAL WITH ASSIGNMENTS

_____ HAS A PLEASANT DISPOSITION

_____ TAKES AN INTEREST IN SCHOOLWORK

_____ ACCEPTS RESPONSIBILITY

_____

_____

TEACHER _____

DATE _____

Document 3.5 Communication with Parents, Alarming Behavior

ALARMING BEHAVIOR

Dear Responsible Adult:

This note is being filled out by me for the following reasons:

_____ 1. I failed to keep my hands, feet, or property in my own space.

_____ 2. I chose to continue disrupting class even after being asked to correct my inappropriate behaviors.

_____ 3. I interrupted instruction by having to be corrected during class time.

_____ 4. I interfered with another student's opportunity to learn by interrupting, talking, or bothering him or her.

_____ 5. I chose to sit in class and waste my own and my teacher's time by not paying attention.

_____ 6. Other: _____

_____

This problem will not continue because I will:

_____

_____

_____ 1. I was warned to correct my behavior and have been in conference with the teacher about my behavior prior to this note home.

_____ 2. My teachers are requesting a parent conference, since I have had a previous problem in this class.

_____ 3. This is the last note to be sent in this form. In the future I will be referred for disciplinary action.

Sincerely,

_____   Telephone No. _____
(Student Name)

Teacher signature: _____   Date: _____

Parent signature: _____

Document 3.6 High School Schoolwide Discipline Plan

At our school we expect all students to behave appropriately while at school and during extracurricular activities. In order to guarantee an excellent learning environment for all students, the following schoolwide discipline plan has been formulated. It is based on the following expectations:

1. No student will interfere with teacher instruction.
2. No student will interfere with another student's learning.
3. No student will engage in any behavior that is not in his/her best interest or in the best interest of others.

I. Schoolwide Rules
(Schoolwide Rules will be in effect at all school activities—on or off campus.)

A. In addition to individual classroom behavioral expectations, students must exhibit polite behavior in assemblies, the library, the cafeteria, the hallways, and on campus grounds.
B. Students will not be permitted to interrupt class without written administrative or faculty approval.
C. Students will not be permitted to bring stereos, walkman-type radios, recorders, televisions, electronic games, beepers or telephones to school. They will be returned to parents or guardians only.
D. Students must be in class prior to the tardy bell or a penalty will be assessed through departmental tardy policies. A schoolwide tardy policy will also be followed.
E. Corridor passes are required any time a student is in the hall after the tardy bell rings. Student aides must visibly display badges which can be substituted for corridor passes.
F. No food or drink will be allowed in classrooms or hallways. Neither candy or gum is to be sold in classrooms. All candy/gum sales should be limited to before school, during lunch, and/or after school.
G. No hats/caps/head coverings are allowed on the school's campus. (This applies to both boys and girls.)
H. Students will refrain from displaying inappropriate physical affection.

I. Students entering a class without permission should be referred to the dean. If they refuse to leave or identify themselves, security will be summoned and an automatic RPC will be issued as soon as their identity is established.
J. Student will discard anything he/she may be drinking or eating before leaving the cafeteria.
K. Hazing or harassing of students will not be tolerated. Any student who subjects other students to abuse, or other acts which tend to disgrace of degrade, is guilty of hazing or harassment.

II. **Immediate Referral to the Dean**

All students are expected to behave in a manner that will be a credit to themselves and our school. When students engage in inappropriate behavior, they will be dealt with fairly and consistently using progressive discipline. Students may be subject to a required parent conference (RPC), out-of-school suspension, arrest, referral to Opportunity School, and/or expulsion (as appropriate) for the following:

1. Fighting (automatic 3-5 day suspension): A second fight in one school year could result in an Opportunity School referral.
2. Assault or physical abuse on any person.
3. Theft, extortion, vandalism, or destruction of school property.
4. The use and/or possession of alcohol or illegal drugs is an automatic referral to school district Drug Program and may result in contact of law enforcement officials and/or referral to Opportunity School.
5. Possession of weapons.
6. Directing obscene, vulgar, profane, or disrespectful language to any staff member.
7. Disruptive classroom behavior.
8. Forging corridor passes, admission slips, medical notes and/or providing any false information on school forms.
9. Failure to identify oneself upon request and/or failure to report to the dean's office when directed to do so by any school personnel.
10. Smoking/use of smokeless tobacco on or near campus.
11. Excessive tardiness.
12. Gambling/card playing.
13. Dress code violation.
14. Gross insubordination.
15. Racial derogatory statements.

III. Dress and Appearance

The high school dress code is in accordance with school district regulation and the specific needs of the school. The specific requirements and prohibitions are:

1. Requires the wearing of shoes.
2. Requires the wearing of shirts or blouses appropriately buttoned. Unbuttoned shirts or blouses are prohibited.
3. Required that all attire BE HEMMED and at least fingertip length. **NO CUTOFFS, NO FRAYED EDGES, AND CANNOT BE TORN OR HAVE HOLES**.
4. Prohibits the wearing of skirts, dresses, and shorts that are not fingertip length.
5. Prohibits the wearing of transparent, see-through, bare midriff shirts/blouses, tank tops, muscle shirts, strapless, low-cut, or open-back clothing.
6. Prohibits the wearing of hats on campus. (This applies to both boys and girls.)
7. Prohibits the wearing of sunglasses in the building. (They must be out of sight.)
8. Prohibits the wearing of gloves, bandannas, spike or studded jewelry, and wallet chains.
9. Prohibits slogans or advertising on clothing, which by their controversial or obscene nature, disrupts the educational setting. This includes any clothing which advertises alcoholic beverages or drugs.
10. Prohibits the sagging of pants or shorts.
11. Prohibits the wearing of any attire that is not conducive to the educational setting at school.

Any student violating the dress code **will not** be allowed to attend class. The principal shall retain authorization to grant exceptions for special occasions and/or conditions.

IV. Drug Education Program

The school district, in conjunction with Juvenile Court Services, sponsors a student/parent drug education program. When a student is under the influence or in possession of a controlled substance on school grounds or at school activities participation in this program is mandatory.

V. Expulsion Regulation
Expulsion shall mean the termination of enrollment as the result of behavior so serious that future attendance in the schools of the district is not contemplated.

Committing these crimes will subject the student to permanent expulsion:

A. <u>Arson</u> - The willful burning of any part of the school building or property therein.
B. <u>Battery</u> - Bodily injury to a school district employee at school or at school-related activities.
C. <u>Controlled Substances</u> - Selling controlled substances or substances represented to be controlled substances.
D. <u>Robbery/Extortion</u> - Taking anything of value from another by use of force.
E. <u>Weapons</u> - Possession, use, transmittal, or concealment of ANY weapon. Weapons are defined as firearms, knives, explosives, inflammable materials or any other items that may cause bodily injury or death.

Students committing the above crimes shall be subject to expulsion and will be prosecuted to the fullest extent of the law.

Opportunity School
Students may be referred to Opportunity School for the following:

A. Continues violation of school rules.
B. Defacing school property
C. Profanity directed toward any staff member.
D. Two fights in one school year.

Required Parent Conference (RPC) Procedure
The student, if present, is called into the dean's office and signs the RPC form.

1. One copy of the RPC is given to the student to take home and one copy is mailed home.
2. Depending upon the nature of the infraction, a student may be allowed to remain in school until the end of the day, or be sent home immediately. The dean issuing the RPC will determine which action will be taken.

3. Upon notification of RPC, the parent must call the school to arrange an appointment with the dean within three days.
4. Following the conference, the student is given an "Admit to Class" pass which must be presented to each teacher.

Smoking/Smokeless Tobacco
Smoking or chewing tobacco is not allowed anywhere on or near the high school campus. This includes the parking lots and the surrounding neighborhood areas. Students found smoking/chewing tobacco in these areas will be subject to a Required Parent Conference and possible suspension.

Suspensions
A notice of suspension will be used in cases of a serious nature when circumstances may warrant further action or investigation. Upon returning to school after a suspension, a student will be allowed (and expected) to make up work missed within a time frame specified by the teacher. While on suspension, a student should not be on school premises or attend any school activities.

Tardiness
All students are expected to be inside their classrooms when the tardy bell rings. Students 30 minutes or more late to class will be marked absent. Students between 10 and 29 minutes late to class will be sent to the dean's office where parent contact will be made and/or the student will be placed on RPC. On the fifth (5th) tardy, students will be sent to the dean's office and automatically RPC'd. All tardies are calculated by the semester. Students are expected to sign unexcused tardy referrals.

Tardy Notebook
Each teacher will provide a tardy notebook for student to sign when entering class after the tardy bell. This notebook is for the protection of the student. The student's signature is proof of his/her presence when reporting to class after attendance has been taken. If the student is tardy and does not sign the book, and is marked absent, THE ABSENCE WILL REMAIN. It is the teacher's responsibility to provide the tardy notebook and the student's responsibility to sign it.

Document 3.7 Detention Notice

Dear Parent:

This notice is to inform you that

_____

has disrupted class by:

_____ annoying fellow students	_____ roaming around the room
_____ not working in class	_____ not having assignment(s)
_____ not bringing materials	_____ excessive tardiness
_____ insubordination	_____ talking incessantly
_____ failing to show for detention	_____ other _____ _____

and must report to room _____ at 7:40 A.M. or 2:30 P.M. on _____ to serve _____

minutes of detention. Your cooperation in this matter is appreciated. If you have any questions, please call. Thank you.

Student's Signature _____

Teacher's Signature _____

Parent's Signature _____

Document 3.8 Referral Form

DEAN REFERRAL

Student Name _____ Grade _____ Student No. _____

Teacher _____ Date _____ Time _____ Period _____

Nature of Problem (Please be as specific as possible):

_____
_____
_____
_____
_____

Previous Action by Teacher: **Date(s):**

_____ One-on-one conference with the student   _____
_____ Telephone contact with the parent   _____
_____ Teacher detention(s)   _____
_____ Counselor referral   _____
_____ Teacher/Parent conference   _____
_____ Other: _____   _____

Action by Dean:

_____ Conference with student (warning and/or reprimand)
_____ Telephone conference with the parent
_____ Required parent conference
_____ Dean's detention
_____ Formal suspension
_____ Other: _____

Dean's Signature _____ Date _____ Time _____

Document 3.9 Classroom Discipline Log

Student's Name _____ Room # _____ Teacher's Name _____

TYPE OF MISBEHAVIOR ( ) _____

Tardiness:								
Disrespect:								
Disruptive (verbal):								
Failure to do assigned work:								
Harassment of other:								
Other:								
Corrective action taken:								
Counseling by teacher:								
Counseling by principal:								
Phone call to parent:								
Letter to parent (U.S. mail):								
Classroom meeting:								
Parent-Teacher conference:								
Other:								
Recorded by: (Initial)								

Key: **C = Classroom**
　　　SG = School Grounds
　　　CF = Cafeteria

Document 3.10 Contract Worksheet

STUDENT _____

TEACHER/PRINCIPAL _____

DATE _____

(X)	TASKS	COMMENTS	(X)
( )	1. Establish and maintain rapport.		
( )	2. Explain the purpose of the meeting.		
( )	3. Explain a contract.		
( )	4. Give an example of a contract.		
( )	5. Ask the student to give an example of a contract; if there is no response, give another example.		
( )	6. Discuss possible tasks.		
( )	7. Teacher suggested tasks: _____ _____ _____ _____		
( )	8. Student suggested tasks: _____ _____ _____ _____		
( )	9. Agree on the task.		
( )	10. Ask the student what activities he/she enjoys and what items he/she wishes to possess.		

Document 3.10 Contract Worksheet, Continued

(X)	TASKS	COMMENTS	(X)
( )	11. Record student-suggested reinforcers.		
( )	12. Identify the time allotted for the task.		
( )	13. Discuss methods of evaluation.		
( )	14. Agree on the method of evaluation.		
( )	15. Restate and clarify the method of evaluation.		
( )	16. Negotiate the delivery of the reinforcer.		
( )	17. Set the date for renegotiation.		
( )	18. Write two copies of the contract.		
( )	19. Read the contract to the student.		
( )	20. Elicit the student's verbal affirmation and give your own affirmation.		
( )	21. Sign the contract and have the student sign it.		
( )	22. Congratulate the student (and yourself).		

DOCUMENT 3.11 BEHAVIOR PROGRESS CARD

BEHAVIOR PROGRESS CARD

STUDENT: _____ DATE _____

subject/time

BEHAVIORS TO CHANGE:
1. _____

2. _____

3. _____

4. _____
   _____

TODAY'S GOAL: _____
TODAY'S TOTAL: _____

COMMENTS:
_____

PARENT'S SIGNATURE: _____
_____

Document 3.12 Behavior Contract

WATCH ME GROW

Here is what I plan to do:

_____

_____

_____

_____

When I do, I'll be able to

_____

_____

And I will have it done by _____

_____ _____
Date   Student

_____ _____
Witness   Teacher

Document 3.13 Behavior Improvement Contract

FOR: _____

        3 POINTS = SUPER   1 POINT = NOT SO GOOD
        2 POINTS = FAIR   0 POINTS = UNSATISFACTORY

Was the student's social behavior acceptable today? (in seat, talking only with permission, respectful to others, nonaggressive)

_____

Did the student pay attention and work on class assignments during class? (assignments handed in)

_____

Did the student hand in the homework assignment that was due today?

_____

Homework: _____

_____

Document 3.14 Team/Student/Parent Conference Summary Form

Date: _____

Student's Name: _____ Grade: _____ Team: _____

Reason for Conference: _____
_____
_____
_____

Parent/Student Concerns: _____
_____
_____
_____

Teacher(s) Concerns: _____
_____
_____
_____

Goals/Recommendations:
   (1) _____
   (2) _____
   (3) _____

Submitted by: _____

Next conference or follow-up: _____

DOCUMENT 3.15 PARENT CONTACT RECORD

Student's Name _____
                     (Last)   (First)   (Middle)

Parent's Name _____
                   (Last)   (First)   (Middle)

Teacher's Name _____ ____ Teacher ____ Returned
                                                              Initiated   Parent Call

1st Attempt ____ ____ Phone Numbers Called _____
           Date Time   Home/Work

2nd Attempt ____ ____ Phone Numbers Called _____
           Date Time   Home/Work

Copy mailed home if there is no telephone. Date mailed: _____

Reasons for the Contact:

___ Good Grades	___ Excessive Absence	___ Detention
___ Good Participation	___ Unprepared for Work	___ Poor Grades
___ Good Conduct	___ No School Supplies	___ Missing Work
___ Good Overall Performance	___ Too Much Talking	___ Tardiness
___ Improving	___ Unacceptable Citizenship	
___ Other _____		

Specific comments regarding reason for contact: _____

_____

_____

Specific outcome(s) of discussion: _____

_____

_____

Parent: If you would like additional information regarding this report, please call the counselor's office to arrange a conference. Thank you.

DOCUMENT 3.16 BEHAVIOR MANAGEMENT SYSTEM FOR SPECIFIC PROBLEMS

Behavior Contract for _____

    The following behavior and consequences have been discussed with his/her parent or guardian. The parent's signature acknowledges receipt and understanding of this system.

    I have been given a copy and participated in a parent/teacher conference regarding my child's management system.

_____   _____
        Parent   Person Discussing System

PRETEACHING/PREBEHAVIOR ACTIVITIES
1. Continual counseling/support regarding appropriate behavior
2. Participation in role-playing situations frustrating to student

AFTER STUDENT ACTS INAPPROPRIATELY
1. Verbal aggression with peer
   a. lose points
   b. removal from group
2. Verbal aggression with adult
   a. lose points
   b. no adult help for activity
   c. removal from room
3. Physical aggression with peer
   a. lose 3 points and in-class suspension if he/she remains nondisruptive
   b. if not nondisruptive, then day suspension building to 3-day suspension
   c. refer to another agency that provides more self-contained/less privileges program
4. Physical aggression with adult (this includes his/her behavior when adult must retrain him or her)
   a. automatic 3-day suspension and possible prosecution for assault
   b. again refer to more restrictive setting

We will work with _____ and provide positive reinforcement for ignoring/or avoiding being involved in all activities listed above.

4

STUDENT GUIDANCE: GUIDANCE AND COUNSELING SERVICES

Any well-trained administrator can identify the primary purpose of public education; it is to teach children and adolescents the necessary skills to become productive citizens in a democratic society. This altruistic goal is instilled in the hearts and lives of educators. Why is it, then, that whenever groups of administrators engage in conversation, the topic does not usually center on teaching skills necessary for an effective democracy but rather on the unique needs of students in today's changing world and how difficult this business of educating students has become? The need for greater social services, counseling, and other support services has become not just a nice frill but an absolute necessity if schools are to address the needs of students.

Early in the history of our country the teaching of reading, writing, mathematics, and history was primarily done through the auspices of value-laden literature and the Bible. It was assumed that the act of schooling, which required dedication and hard work, would produce productive, responsible citizens. The family and church provided any additional training deemed necessary related to values, integrity, and social development.

As society has changed, so has the structure of the family, and as a result children of today come to school with many different needs and concerns. Educators have come to realize that while the goal of public education historically remains the same, the task has changed dramatically. It is not the intent of this chapter to describe the woes of society that have contributed to the changing needs of students but rather to focus on ways in which schools might address the needs of students through guidance and counseling programs and to identify the role of the administrator in accessing and utilizing such services.

SCHOOL-BASED GUIDANCE AND COUNSELING PROGRAMS

How do school administrators deal with the reality of school-based guidance and counseling programs when their status is constantly changing? One year there will be a big push from the state level or district level with a verbalized commitment to place counselors in all schools and then funds fall short, test scores drop, and money is pulled from the counseling pool and placed toward other priorities. If administrators are put in a position of having to choose between hiring an assistant principal or a counselor, many will choose the counselor because there are so many students in need of counseling services. There is really no debate that the need for such services is critical; however, it is equally critical that principals understand the role of such services in order to use them effectively. Just for clarification, a brief description will be provided in this chapter of the basic components of school-based guidance programs and how the elementary, middle, and high school counselor's roles differ.

School-based guidance and counseling programs are designed to address the needs of students by helping them gain knowledge of self and others, and to provide direction related to educational and vocational development. Such programs provide a system designed to anticipate and facilitate the educational, career, and personal/social needs of students.

School-based guidance and counseling programs are built around four basic components: 1) Guidance curriculum, 2) Individual planning, 3) Responsive services, and 4) Systems support. Most school districts that have a Guidance and Counseling Department develop a K–12 Guidance curriculum that systematically outlines activities and expectations for introducing students to knowledge of normal growth and development. In schools with counselors the guidance curriculum is primarily taught through classroom activities or introduced in small group activities. As an administrator it is important that you work closely with your school counselor to establish guidelines related to class/small group activities. When a counseling program is first introduced at a school teachers and parents are sometimes hesitant to utilize the services and often the counselor has plenty of time to address requests and establish programs. Then, after a few months, the counselor is inundated with requests and it becomes difficult to establish priorities. The administrator and counselor must work together to communicate to parents, teachers, and students about the basic components of the counseling program and to establish priorities based on the unique needs of the school. The basic components of most school-based counseling and guidance programs also include individual planning, responsive services, and systems support.

Individual planning entails working with individual students to assist them in planning, monitoring, and managing their own learning as well as their personal and career development. Counselors often help students evaluate their educational, occupational, and personal goals. At the elementary level counselors often work with students who need to develop study skills and learn how to organize their time. At the secondary level counselors work with students in using personal/social, educational, career and labor market information in planning personal, educational, and occupational goals. Through individual planning, counselors assist students in making the transition from school to school, school to work, or work to additional education and training.

Responsive services provided by counselors are often student-initiated and deal with specific concerns requiring counseling, consultation, referral, or just additional information. Counselors are frequently required to provide assistance following an emergency situation or crisis with a student. Such services are usually short-term and temporary. In most cases of very serious situations or those requiring long-term services, the counselor uses outside referral resources.

Systems support is an important aspect of any school-based counseling program. Systems support for counselors includes participating in staff development opportunities, interacting with support agencies within the community, consulting with teachers, and knowing about current trends in the area of guidance and counseling.

ROLE OF THE ELEMENTARY SCHOOL COUNSELOR

The primary role of the elementary school counselor is one of intervention and prevention related to problems that interfere with the ability of children to achieve their greatest academic, social, and personal potential. Elementary school counselors usually work with students K through 5 or K through 6 providing a wide range of activities and services. Such services usually include classroom guidance activities, individual or group counseling, parent education, parent and teacher consultation, referrals to community agencies, and crisis intervention. Elementary counselors work under the premise that if a student's problem can be addressed and remediated during the elementary school years the student stands a greater chance of successfully coping with the unique demands placed on adolescents at the middle school and senior high school levels.

ROLE OF THE MIDDLE SCHOOL COUNSELOR

Middle school counselors are responsible for providing a guidance and counseling program that addresses the unique needs of the student in grades 6 through 8. Recognizing that peer relationships and social interactions are paramount in the life of young adolescents, the middle school counselor must work equally with students, teachers, and parents in an attempt to help each understand the other. Responsibilities of the middle school counselor also include:

- ♦ providing orientation activities for the incoming grade and other new students
- ♦ guiding eighth grade students in the development of their high school four-year plan

- assisting new students entering school after the school year begins with course selection
- interpreting standardized test results information to students, parents, and teachers
- conducting counseling sessions related to specific needs of individuals or groups of students
- consulting with teachers, parents, and staff regarding meeting developmental needs of students
- referring students and parents to in-district or community services and resources

ROLE OF THE SENIOR HIGH SCHOOL COUNSELOR

Senior high school counselors assume primary responsibility for providing guidance and counseling regarding educational and career decisions for students in grades 9 through 12. Most senior high guidance and counseling curriculums include similar components to the elementary and middle school levels with regard to providing counseling services to individuals or groups based on need; however, in most high school settings this part of the curriculum is secondary to career and college placement counseling.

Most school districts identify the primary duties of the senior high school counselor as:

- providing orientation activities for students new to the school
- guiding ninth and tenth graders in planning their high school four-year plan
- assisting eleventh and twelfth graders in evaluating their current status regarding high school graduation, guiding twelfth graders and assisting them in developing and taking appropriate steps toward implementing their post-high school education and/or career plans
- collaborating with middle school counselors in pre-registration of eighth graders

- interpreting standardized test results information to students, parents, and teachers
- guiding students in the application of the test results information to their educational and career plans
- planning and conducting supervision of career education activities
- providing a mechanism for the systematic and efficient dissemination of current, accurate information needed by individual students and/or parents as they develop their education or career plans

Secondary counselors assume responsibility for assisting students in planning for high school graduation as well as planning post-secondary training options. Often school districts develop graduate profile planning guides that are designed to assist students in systematically planning toward graduation and beyond. Such guides frequently include information related to:

- high school graduation requirements
- options for high school programs of study
- career systems and career clusters
- academic calendar for parents and students
- tips on gathering information about plans after high school
- trades apprenticeship programs
- military opportunities
- trade and technical schools
- testing for university admission
- financial aid and scholarships

ADVANTAGES OF SCHOOL-BASED GUIDANCE AND COUNSELING PROGRAMS

As an administrator you may have a gut-level feeling that things are better as a result of having a school counselor, but sometimes it helps to have those feelings verified. For example, the following excerpts are from a letter written to the administrator by parents who had been attending an afternoon parenting class conducted by the school counselor.

> We would like to take this time to ask that the class be continued throughout the school year. All parents that have been attending are willing to contribute financially in order to keep it going. This class not only opened new doors for us as parents but also made for some great family time. Ms. Baxter's class has helped us accept we are only human and no child is born with a book of instructions. We feel very fortunate that we are able to receive this kind of assistance at the school. School personnel is to be commended for recognizing the need to provide support for students but also for the parents of students.

Effective school-based guidance and counseling programs provide support to students, parents, and teachers. Educators readily agree that an effective counseling program enhances the overall instructional program and provides much needed assistance to students in need of support. Administrators understand that the impact of such programs are far-reaching and the advantages are many; however, schools and school districts are called upon frequently to defend the need for such services.

Some of the benefits and advantages of school-based guidance and counseling programs for educational and community stakeholders are identified in Figure 4.1. This list might be used by an administrator to support and justify the need for such a program.

Many schools that have an assigned counselor organize a Guidance Advisory Board that plans and organizes the guidance program based on the needs of the school. The primary function of the Guidance Advisory Board is to establish a formal communication link between the various groups being serviced by the guidance program and the program itself. The board serves as a channel for information, understanding, and program interpretation for students, parents, teachers, and the

FIGURE 4.1 BENEFITS AND ADVANTAGES OF SCHOOL-BASED GUIDANCE AND COUNSELING PROGRAMS

For Students
1. Develops understanding of self and others
2. Develops problem-solving and decision-making skills
3. Promotes knowledge and assistance in educational and career development
4. Makes students aware of available support systems
5. Broadens knowledge of a changing world
6. Increases chances for successful educational experience
7. Encourages the development of positive, supportive relationships

For Parent
1. Provides a system of support for parents regarding their child's educational development
2. Assists parents in accessing special services and community resources
3. Develops a home-school communication network
4. Maintains a system for a child's long-range planning

For Teachers
1. Encourages collegiality and communication among staff and faculty
2. Provides a team effort in addressing problems and concerns
3. Produces a sense of support
4. Assists teachers in knowing available services and resources
5. Provides for a systematic avenue of accessing information

For the Business Community
1. Provides opportunity for collaboration between the business and educational community

2. Increases opportunities for business, industry, and labor to participate actively in the total school program
3. Provides a potential workforce with decision-making skills, preemployment skills, and increased worker maturity
4. Promotes dialogue between the world of work and schools in determining curriculum and academic needs

For the University and College System
1. Provides a means for educational counseling regarding higher education
2. Assists student decision making by making available information related to college entrance expectancies
3. Provides a systematic plan for disseminating information to students and parents
4. Assists in screening potential candidates for admission purposes

For Boards of Education
1. Provides rationale for including a comprehensive guidance program in the school system
2. Provides program information to district personnel
3. Provides ongoing information about student competencies attained through the guidance program efforts
4. Creates communication and collaboration with parents regarding educational issues

For Administrators
1. Provides program structure with specific content and goals
2. Assists in meeting social, emotional, and educational needs of students through a systematic plan for guidance and counseling
3. Increases home-school communication and provides a support for parents and teachers in working with students
4. Maintains access to available support services through the school district and community

administration. The Guidance Advisory Board does such things as:

- assist in determining needs
- assist with planning and implementing various activities and programs
- serve as a public relations agent
- assist with scheduling events and activities
- provide resources for specific activities
- maintain consistent communication between those involved in the counseling program and school personnel
- assist in accessing community resources

INDIVIDUAL/GROUP GUIDANCE AND COUNSELING

School guidance counselors at all levels generally offer a variety of individual and/or group counseling services. Such programs are based on specific needs that have been identified by students, teachers, or parents. Sometimes groups emerge as a result of a crisis or tragedy. Group sessions may be ongoing throughout the year or may be for only one or two sessions. Listed below are counseling groups that are frequently offered by school counselors:

- Banana Splits Club (any change in family status, divorce, death of parent, etc.)
- Dealing with Anger
- Fear of School
- Study Skills
- Character Building
- Friendship or Peer Relationships
- Decision-Making Skills
- Mainstreaming or Inclusion Issues
- Socialization

Guidance and Counseling Services

- Dealing with Being Different (handicapped, overweight, etc.)
- Dealing with Abuse (physical, alcohol, sex)
- Dealing with the Death of a Sibling and/or Parent
- Fitting in at a New School
- My Teacher Hates Me Syndrome
- Everyone Is Always Picking on Me

Referring Students for Counseling Services

Guidelines regarding referring students for guidance and counseling services vary from school to school. Each school must decide on an efficient referral process that includes appropriate notification of parents, is easily accessible to students and staff, and allows the counselor to maintain records and track counseling referrals. It is suggested that the process be as simple as possible. Many counselors use referral forms that include academic and behavior checklists, others just ask for brief information regarding the reason for the referral. Documents 4.1–4.4 located at the end of the chapter are sample counseling referral forms used by schools.

Schools Without a Counselor

Many schools are faced with providing assistance to parents and students without the aid of a school counselor, particularly at the elementary school level or in rural schools. In such cases the site administrator must work with school personnel to identify and access programs and resources outside the school setting that are available to address academic and social concerns of students. There are a variety of commercial programs that have been created to assist schools in developing student self-responsibility. Many of these programs are used by school counselors in school-based guidance and counseling programs, but are also available to and have been effectively used by schools that do not have a formal guidance and counseling program. Four such programs will be described in this section, Skills For Growing, Self Management Program, Tribes: A Process for Social Development and Cooperative Learning, and Positive Action.

Skills For Growing, published by Lions Quest International, is a positive youth development program for grades K through 5 that grew out of concerns over an ever-changing society that competes with the family as a source of children's values and ideas. The program is an attempt to respond to the needs of families by:

- helping children develop positive social behavior that includes self-discipline, responsibility, and good judgment. It also supports the ability to get along with others as a key to being successful in today's world.
- helping students develop positive commitments to family, school, peers, and communities. An emphasis on leading healthy drug-free lives is communicated throughout the program.

The program consists of a teacher's manual at each grade level and student-family activity books entitled *Together Times*. Staff development is required to promote consistency and continuity in program implementation. Lessons are designed to be presented two times a week for thirty to forty-five minutes with themes that are coordinated throughout all the grade levels.

The Skills For Growing curriculum may be integrated into other subject areas; it is particularly relevant to the areas of social studies and health. Goals and objectives are written for each unit and included in the teacher's manual, which also provides strategies, resources, and other activities to support each teaching unit. For additional information regarding this program contact:

Skills For Growing
Lions Quest Programs
Quest International Headquarters
1984 Coffman Road
P.O. Box 566
Newark, Ohio 43055
1-800-446-2700

Another program that has been published for use in schools is the Self Management Program written by Gene Bedley. This program deals directly with teaching children to solve their own problems. The Self Management Program may be used in the administrator's office, in the classroom, or at home to assist students in solving problems. Teachers have found the program helpful in solving those after-lunch-recess playground disputes that often end up back in the classroom. This program has also been used to train student mediators in resolving playground problems. Booklets on specific problems (fighting, playing unfairly, lying, talking back, etc.) are included, as well as charts designed to track responsibilities and goals.

Mr. Bedley has written this program with input from children who have been successful in learning to solve their problems in constructive ways. Administrators have found this program helpful by having students work through each booklet, which reinforces positive ways to deal with individual problems. For more information regarding this program contact:

Self Management Program
People-Wise Publication
14252 East Mall
Irvine, California 92714
(714) 551-6690

Tribes: A Process for Social Development and Cooperative Learning is a K through adult program developed by Jeanne Gibbs that has been successfully implemented at schools both with and without counselors. The program utilizes the basics of relatedness, respect, and responsibility to promote a positive learning environment. Reviewing research, Jeanne Gibbs (1987) found that:

- positive peer regard improves self-image
- cooperative peer teaching and learning methods lead to higher test scores
- positive classroom climate enhances motivation and improves behavior

Lessons and activities are developed that provide students and adults the opportunity to learn strategies to solve problems individually and in group situations. The Tribes norms include attentive listening, no put-downs, the right to pass, and confidentiality. The norms are practiced in meaningful situations and become part of the expected classroom standards. Teachers who have incorporated the Tribes philosophy in their classrooms have found that students interact more positively with each other and are more confident about themselves.

Training in the use of the Tribes Program must be provided by a trained facilitator. For further information contact:

TRIBES
Jeanne Gibbs
Center for Human Development
391 Taylor Blvd., Suite 120
Pleasant Hill, CA 94523
(510) 687-8844

Dr. Carol Gerber-Allred developed Positive Action, a comprehensive self-concept program for students in grades K through 8. It is designed to help students change their behavior while transforming school climate. Based on research conducted by the United States Education Department, Positive Action has been used to prevent drug abuse, school dropout, and teen pregnancies, and has been used to teach good health habits including building a healthy self-concept. Dr. Gerber-Allred began Positive Action in 1973 and has continued to expand and enhance the program.

The Positive Action classroom curriculum contains approximately 140 daily lessons in grades K through 6, and about 80 daily lessons for grades 7 and 8. Lessons are designed to be presented four times a week for approximately fifteen minutes and are coordinated throughout each grade level. It is intended that the Positive Action program extend throughout the school through the involvement of the principal, teachers, support staff, and parents. The Principal's Manual provides information on how to set up the program for students, staff, and parents, and contains resources such as stickers, tokens, and certificates to use as incentives and positive reinforcement.

Schools that have used the Positive Action program report that it is easy to implement, provides continuity throughout the school, and provides parents with pertinent information about how to support the program at home. For further information contact:

Positive Action
Carol Gerber-Allred, Ph.D.
321 Eastland Drive
Twin Falls, Idaho
(208) 733-1328

In addition to commercially developed programs there are many strategies and activities that a school without a counselor may incorporate to provide guidance and assistance to students. Forming an ad hoc committee made up of teachers, parents, and community leaders to research and identify available resources within the community is a beginning. The following ideas have been successfully implemented at some schools where school-based guidance and counseling services are limited or nonexistent.

- Adult mentors trained and assigned to work specifically with students who are in need of assistance, behaviorally or academically
- Schoolwide intervention teams that work directly with teachers in identifying strategies for addressing behavior or academic problems
- Ongoing staff development related to recognizing and reporting student concerns such as child abuse, ADD/ADHD, substance abuse, depression, suicide, etc.
- Training office staff to alert administration of attendance problems, change in family status, custody issues
- Maintaining a Community Resource Guide for teachers and parents
- Organizing districtwide parenting conferences with community support groups presenting sessions on parenting issues

- Developing partnerships with businesses and other community agencies
- Providing Brown Bag dialogue sessions at lunchtime for parents in downtown business areas or apartment complexes
- Parent breakfast clubs held monthly as a means for presenting information on parenting issues and maintaining dialogue
- Inviting community support groups to hold their meetings at the school
- Writing grants to fund special tutoring and intervention programs
- Working with senior citizen groups to access adult volunteers to work in the schools

Tremendous resources are available to schools without counselors through agencies and organizations within the community whose job it is to work with children and parents. Many such agencies receive public funding and are very willing to work with school personnel.

Parent Education Classes

Parenting classes offered through the school district or sponsored by individual schools build a partnership between home and school. School counselors frequently coordinate the organization of parent education classes. Counselors sometimes provide the instruction and at other times enlist experts in the field to teach classes. For schools without counselors, community agencies, juvenile court services, and social work agencies often provide parenting classes free of charge and are often willing to hold their classes at local schools. Clusters of schools may work together to organize and plan for ongoing parenting classes.

Successful parenting classes must be practical and relevant to the needs of those attending. Classes usually run three to six weeks, with classes meeting once a week. Small groups of fifteen to twenty persons seem to work better than larger groups. Possible topics for ongoing parenting classes include:

- Communicating with Teenagers
- Helping My Child Deal with ADD/ADHD
- Parenting in the 90s
- Teaching Children Responsibility and Regard
- Children from Zero to Five
- Parenting Techniques That Help Children Be Successful Students
- What to Do Besides Yelling, Screaming, and Sending Them to Their Room
- How to Be a Parent Without Losing Your Mind
- Discipline: It Is a Four-Letter Word—LOVE
- Helping Siblings Live Harmoniously
- To Spank or Not to Spank
- We Are What We Hear—Parent/Child Communication
- The Do's and Don'ts of Time Out

SUMMARY

School-based guidance and counseling programs are built on the premise that building a boy or girl is far easier than mending a man or a woman. School counselors play a vital role in helping schools provide for the developmental needs of students, socially and academically. A well-developed guidance curriculum that begins in the elementary school and is carried on through middle school and high school helps students to become successful problem solvers and participate in decisions related to their education.

While the task of providing guidance and counseling to students may be more challenging for the school that does not have an assigned school counselor, it is not impossible. Accessing community resources can assist schools in providing needed services to students and parents.

The site administrator must assume responsibility for coordinating the school-based guidance and counseling program if one exists, or leading the search for available resources and services if the school does not have a counselor. The needs of students and parents is too great for the administrator to adopt an "Oh, well, what can I do?" attitude. The school administrator must become aggressive in knocking on the doors of universities, social services, and members of the business community to present to them the need as well as a plan for their involvement in the schools.

FOLLOW-UP ACTIVITIES

1. Make a list of the social service agencies, private hospitals, and counseling programs that are listed in the phone book. Contact those on the list to determine the scope of their services and begin to create a resource book of available services. Particularly note those agencies that provide free services or payment based on ability to pay.
2. Develop a parent survey designed to determine interest in parenting classes. It is usually wise to identify some possible topics for classes and let parents identify those in which they are interested.
3. Review the basic components of a school-based guidance and counseling program and identify how a school without a counselor might address the different components: Guidance Curriculum, Individual Planning, Responsive Services, Systems Support.

RESOURCES

Act Against Violence
Community Resource Guide
Thirteen/WNET
P.O. Box 245
Little Falls, New Jersey 07414-9876

American Schools Counseling Association
5999 Stevenson Ave.
Alexandria, Virginia 22304-3300
(703) 823-9800
FAX (703) 461-3569

Beginning Alcohol and Addiction Basic Education Studies
33 East Forest
Detroit, Michigan 48201
1-800-54-BABES

Big Brothers/Big Sisters of America
230 North Thirteenth St.
Philadelphia, Pennsylvania 19107
(215) 222-4441

Boys and Girls Clubs of America
Gang Intervention Services
1230 W. Peachtree St. NW
Atlanta, Georgia 30309
(404) 892-3317

Childhelp USA
P.O. Box 630
Los Angeles, California 90029
1-800-4A CHILD

Children's Creative Response to Conflict
Box 271
521 N. Broadway
Nyack, New York 10960
(914) 353-1796

Committee for Children
2203 Airport Way South, Ste. 500
Seattle, Washington 98134-2027
1-800-634-4449

National Association for Mediation Education (NAME)
205 Hampshire House, Box 33635
University of Massachusetts
Amherst, Massachusetts 01003
(413) 545-2462

National Clearinghouse for Alcohol and Drug Information
11426-28 Rockville Pike
Rockville, Maryland 20852
1-800-729-6686

National Clearinghouse on Child Abuse and Neglect Information
P.O. Box 1182
Washington, D.C. 20013-1182
(703) 385-7565

National Committee to Prevent Child Abuse
332 S. Michigan Ave. Ste 1600
Chicago, Illinois 60604-4347
(312) 663-3520

National Institute on Alcohol Abuse and Alcoholism
6000 Executive Blvd. MSC 7003
Bethesda, Maryland 20892-7003
(301) 443-3885

Office of Substance Abuse Prevention
NIDA
Parklawn Bld. 5600
Fischer Lane Room 10A39
Rockville, Maryland 20857
(301) 443-6245

Parent Resource Institute for Drug Education, Inc.
3610 De Kalb Technology Parkway
Suite 105
Atlanta, Georgia 30340
1-800-853-7867

The Peace Education Foundation, Inc.
1900 Biscayne Blvd.
Miami, Florida 33132
(305) 576-5075

Positive Action
Carol Berber-Allred, Ph.D.
321 Eastland Drive
Twin Falls, Idaho 83301
(208) 733-1328

Self Management Program
People-Wise Publication
14252 East Mall
Irvine, California 92714
(714) 551-6690

Skills for Growing
Lions Quest Programs
Quest International Headquarters
1984 Coffman Road
Newark, Ohio 43055
1-800-446-2700

Tribes
Jeanne Gibbs
Center for Human Development
391 Taylor Blvd., Suite 120
Pleasant Hill, California 94523
(510) 687-8844

DOCUMENT 4.1 STUDENT APPOINTMENT REQUEST

Dear Counselor,

    I would like to make an appointment with you. I need help with:

        _____ a problem at school

        _____ a problem with friends

        _____ a problem at home

        _____ other_____

Name _____

Date _____ Homeroom _____

DOCUMENT 4.2 COUNSELING REFERRAL FORM

Student's name: _____ Room # _____

Referred by: _____

Reason for referral: _____

_____

_____

_____

_____

GUIDANCE AND COUNSELING SERVICES 121

DOCUMENT 4.3 COUNSELING REFERRAL

Student's Name:_____Grade: _____
Referral Date: _____Referred By: _____

Please check relevant items:

ACADEMIC PERFORMANCE
_____ Decline in quality of work
_____ Decline in grades earned
_____ Incomplete work
_____ Work not handed in
_____ Failing in this subject

CLASSROOM PERFORMANCE
_____ Disruptive in class
_____ Inattentiveness
_____ Lack of concentration
_____ Lack of motivation
_____ Sleeping in class
_____ Impaired memory
_____ Extreme negativism
_____ In-school absenteeism, skipping class
_____ Late to class
_____ Defiance of authority, breaking the rules
_____ Frequently needs discipline
_____ Cheating
_____ Fighting
_____ Throwing objects
_____ Verbally abusive
_____ Obscene language, gestures
_____ Sudden outbursts
_____ Vandalism
_____ Frequent visits to nurse, counselor
_____ Frequent visits to lavatory
_____ Hyperactivity, nervousness

OTHER BEHAVIORS
_____ Erratic day-to-day behavior
_____ Change in friends and/or peer group
_____ Sudden, unexplained popularity
_____ Mood swings

Document 4.3 Counseling Referral, Continued

_____ Seeks constant adult contact
_____ Seeks adult advise without a specific reason
_____ Time disorientation
_____ Apparent changes in personal values
_____ Depression
_____ Defensiveness
_____ Withdrawal, a loner, separate from others
_____ Other students express concern about a possible problem
_____ Fantasizing, daydreaming
_____ Compulsive over achievement, preoccupied with success
_____ Perfectionism
_____ Difficulty in accepting mistakes
_____ Rigid obedience
_____ Talks freely about drug use, bragging
_____ Associates with known drug users

POSSIBLE ALCOHOL OR DRUG ABUSE (SPECIFIC BEHAVIOR)

Witnessed	Suspected	
_____	_____	Selling, delivering
_____	_____	Possession of alcohol, drugs
_____	_____	Possession of drug paraphanalia
_____	_____	Use of alcohol, drugs
_____	_____	Intoxication
_____	_____	Physical signs, symptoms

What actions have you already taken? (e.g., shared concern and data with student, initiated consequences, parent contact) _____

_____

_____

_____

Any additional comments: _____

_____

_____

_____

GUIDANCE AND COUNSELING SERVICES

DOCUMENT 4.4 COUNSELING REFERRAL

STUDENT _____

DATE _____ REFERRED BY _____

ACADEMIC ISSUES
_____ Failing the course
_____ Lack of interest
_____ Poor use of study time
_____ Not completing assigned work

BEHAVIOR ISSUES
_____ Classroom disruption
Specific comments about behavior:
_____
_____
_____

THE FOLLOWING STEPS WERE TAKEN BY THE TEACHER TO CORRECT THE PROBLEM(S):

1. One-to-one conference with student (date of conference) _____
2. Parent contacted by phone (date of phone contact)_____
3. Teacher/Parent conference (date) _____
4. Teacher/Student/Counselor conference (date)_____

COUNSELOR ACTION TAKEN TO CORRECT THE PROBLEM:

Date: _____ Time: _____

Action:_____
_____
_____
_____

_____   _____
Student's Signature   Counselor's Signature

This is to be signed by the parent and returned to the counselor's office within two days.

_____
Parent's Signature

Dear Parents:
  Please write any comments on the back of this form. If you would like a conference with the teacher or counselor, please call the counseling office at _____.

Thank you!

5

STUDENT GUIDANCE: STUDENT ACTIVITY PROGRAMS

Self-concept, or self-esteem, is an important area of personal and social development for students, as highlighted in the developmental stages described in Chapter 1. This is greatly influenced by experiences at home, with peers, and at school. Elementary children have many experiences during the school day to interact with students their own age as most classrooms are self-contained by ages; they also have opportunities to interact with others during lunch recess, scouting activities, PTA–sponsored activities, etc. Secondary students also have an opportunity to interact before and after school and during the transition time between classes with their peers.

Clubs, organizations, and sports can provide further avenues for children to develop a positive self-concept while providing acceptance, a key word with regard to personal and social development. During the formative years, the peer group takes on added importance. Memberships in groups appear to promote feelings of self-worth and acceptance. Clubs and organizations present situations where, depending on the developmental stage of the child, he or she may find acceptance or a chance to explore areas of strength and interest, while interacting with different groups of people.

Within our changing society, children are spending more time before and after school at day care centers, with babysitters, or at home alone. Many schools at both the elementary and secondary level are also providing such services before or after school, as well as during the school day to meet childcare needs.

At the elementary level, communities have developed day care programs located at the school site run by teachers or instructional aides. In one district, these programs are sponsored by the city's Park and Recreation Department and are known as Safekey. Day care is provided before and after school at the school site. Although this time is mainly used to complete homework, play games or for other activities, several of the school centers have added computer time, math/reading tutoring, or other instructional outlets. More information about the Safekey program may be found in the Resources section at the end of this chapter.

In some school districts, foreign language programs are being implemented before or after school and occur approximately two to three times a week for forty-five minutes. These classes, for the most part, are sponsored by outside agencies and are open to all elementary students on a paying basis. Secondary schools offer Early Bird classes that allow students to take additional classes or add credits to their schedules.

Usually within an elementary school, Student Council programs are set up depending on the needs of the school. Student Councils allow students to participate in the democratic process and give them an idea of how such organizations work. Some schools include all grade levels, first through fifth, while others focus on the intermediate grades. A teacher usually facilitates the program, meeting before school or during lunch. Students may hold offices by campaigning and holding elections with the student population voting for each office. Often at the elementary level, Student Council representatives are chosen by each class and serve as a liaison with officers chosen by the teacher advisor.

Student Council/Government programs are encouraged at the secondary level and function through class officers at each grade. The Student Council at the high school level is the primary student governing organization of the school and is composed of elected student body officers. These usually include

Student Body President, First Vice-President in charge of clubs and dances, Second Vice-President in charge of activities and assemblies, Secretary, and Treasurer, in addition to an Executive Council (members from junior and senior classes, and class officers) and advisory board members. Teachers serve as faculty representatives, monitoring and advising students. Resources and available publications regarding Student Council can be found on page 133.

ELEMENTARY CLUBS AND ORGANIZATIONS

Most elementary activities are organized by teachers or parent volunteers and occur before school, during lunch, or after school. Grants are available that promote such activities, especially for at-risk students or special-needs students.

Clubs, performing groups, and organizations that have been successfully implemented at the elementary level are listed below with a brief description of each. This list is certainly not inclusive of all the activities that might be implemented, again based on the needs of individual schools. As in all cases, administrators need to reflect on the need for such activity, the amount of instructional time that is missed (if any), who will be the responsible party, and how the activity will benefit students. Some of these activities are derived from already existing programs (such as choir and art clubs), while some provide enrichment or remedial assistance.

Choir. This performing group meets under the direction of a music teacher, usually before school or during lunchtime. The goal is to involve students in the beginning levels of chorus, performing for parents or for the community. Most choirs consist of students from fourth and fifth grade.

Art. Many schools provide students the opportunity to learn more about design through a before-school program or at lunch clubs sponsored by teachers. These may be set up by grade levels or by a specific topic (line drawings, portraits, weaving, etc.). The art club often assists the choir by making stage decorations for production numbers.

Computer. Primary and intermediate students meet at different times during the week to learn more about computers. Activities might include word processing, logo, or using software that promotes the curriculum. Computer clubs provide an excellent opportunity for developing partnerships with local businesses.

Chess. Many schools have set up lunchtime chess clubs with tournament play within the school and between schools. Parent volunteers often direct this club and help children learn the fundamentals of the game. There are national chess organizations that sponsor competitions for individuals and schools.

Foreign Language. These clubs are created to provide students with opportunities to learn a language or to become familiar with the culture of a country. At most elementary schools, the languages include Spanish, French, and/or Japanese.

We think it is important to take a close look at the purpose and importance of activities and clubs. With many of our students coming from at-risk homes where there is not much active involvement with these types of activities, we feel that sponsoring clubs and activities helps balance the lives of many of our students.

SECONDARY SCHOOL CLUBS AND ORGANIZATIONS

Middle schools, junior highs, and high schools offer an abundance of clubs, performing groups, and athletic programs for students. Some of these programs that have been nationally or locally developed are listed here with a brief description of each. Other clubs may be organized, depending on the interest of the students, size of the population, or expertise of the teachers. Clubs provide opportunities for students to serve their community, gain leadership responsibilities, or be involved in planning and organizing school events. Many of the clubs help students develop an interest in a career field or provide them with an opportunity to try something new. As indicated previously, most of the clubs and organizations are held before or after school and have at least one teacher sponsor. More information about each type of club and how to organize and monitor may be found on page 133.

CLUBS/ORGANIZATIONS

Name of Club	Description of Club
AMNESTY INTERNATIONAL	This club promotes human rights throughout the world by writing letters protesting violations of human rights.
ART	The purpose of this club is to foster the pursuit of art, further creative abilities, bring art to the attention of students, staff, and community; and to motivate students who show outstanding ability.
CHESS	The chess club provides an opportunity for students to play competitive chess and is open to all levels.
CLOSE UP	This is an organization for junior and senior students interested in the governmental process and how it functions. An annual trip to Washington, D.C., is part of the activities.
COMPUTER CLUB	Open to students having an interest in computers and a desire to learn more about them, the computer club offers students a way to focus on technology.
DISTRIBUTIVE EDUCATION CLUBS OF AMERICA (DECA)	This national organization is for marketing students who may be planning a career in management, sales, advertising, etc.
FOREIGN LANGUAGE	These clubs are created for any student interested in the culture of the French, German, and Spanish speaking world.
FORENSICS	Students debate in competitions locally or out of state, promoting speaking skills.
FUTURE BUSINESS LEADERS OF AMERICA (FBLA)	This national organization is open to students who are enrolled in business-related classes. FBLA promotes a better understanding of business and community interactions.
FUTURE EDUCATORS OF AMERICA (FEA)	This national organization strives to interest students in education as a profession through their school experiences.
FUTURE FARMERS OF AMERICA (FFA)	This national organization strives to interest students in agricultural and animal husbandry.

FUTURE HOMEMAKERS OF AMERICA (FHA)	This is a vocational youth organization for students who are enrolled in home economics courses. Members develop leadership skills as well as participate in various events.
GLOBAL LAB	Students investigate environmental problems and social/political issues through a network of schools in over twenty-one countries linked by computer modems.
HELPING YOU, HELPING ME	This is a tutorial program that enables students to go to elementary schools and work with younger students. (See Chapter 2 for more details.)
INTERACT	Sponsored by the Rotary Club, this international organization provides an opportunity for students to work together in a world fellowship dedicated to service and international understanding.
INTERNATIONAL	The purpose of this club is to create a feeling of unity among students, recognizing the importance of cultural diversity.
J.E.T.S.	J.E.T.S. was developed to promote engineering, technology, mathematics, and science among high school students. Completion of geometry and biology are required for membership.
KEY CLUB	This is an international organization of students committed to school and community service, sponsored by the Kiwanis Club.
MU ALPHA THETA (MATH)	Mu Alpha Theta is a national high school mathematics club to promote scholarship in and enjoyment and understanding of mathematics.
NATIONAL HONOR SOCIETY	This club was created to stimulate academic achievement, a desire to render service, promote worthy leadership, and encourage character development.
S.T.A.T.U.S./S.A.D.D.	This organization's primary goal is to discourage and prevent students from drinking and driving, as well as to say no to any forms of substance abuse.
VARSITY QUIZ	This is an inter-school scholastic competition where selection of team members is based on the results of a written test, an audition in a simulated game, and academic eligibility.

Student Activity Programs

In addition, secondary schools have several publications such as a newspaper and yearbook that are composed and written by students.

Performing Groups

Name of Club	Description of Club
VOCATIONAL INDUSTRIAL CLUBS OF AMERICA (VICA)	VICA was created for students interested in architecture or drafting. Students wishing to compete in the National VICA portion of the club must maintain a 2.00 GPA.
DRILL TEAM/SHORT FLAGS	These teams promote school spirit while performing with the marching band or performing independently.
MUSIC/INSTRUMENTAL	The band program (symphonic and concert) performs and competes locally and out of state. Groups meet daily during regularly scheduled classes.
MUSIC/VOCAL	These programs center around concert choir and glee clubs and meet on a regular basis during the school day. Performances and competitions are arranged throughout the school year.
THESPIANS	This organization promotes interest in performing arts, supporting school drama productions and engaging in fund raisers.
VARSITY SPIRIT LEADERS (CHEERLEADERS)	Organized to promote school spirit and provide support for all athletic groups, varsity spirit leaders usually consist of eleventh and twelfth grade students.
JUNIOR VARSITY CHEERLEADERS	Cheerleaders help promote spirit for junior varsity sports while also performing at school assemblies.
FRESHMAN CHEERLEADERS	This organization promotes and supports freshman sports and performs at school assemblies.
PIN PALS	Pin Pals is a group of students whose purpose is to support the wrestling team at all matches, tournament, activities, and fund raisers.

ATHLETIC PROGRAMS

Athletic programs are a vital part of most secondary schools and are organized by budget allocation. Depending on the size of a school and funds available, athletic programs may include Varsity, Junior Varsity, and Freshman programs for both men and women. The most commonly sponsored teams are:

MEN	WOMEN
Cross Country	Cross Country
Tennis	Tennis
Soccer	Soccer
Golf	Golf
Volleyball	Volleyball
Basketball	Basketball
Baseball	Softball
Swimming	Swimming
Wrestling	
Football	

Athletic programs may be based on try-outs and academic eligibility.

SUMMARY

Clubs, organizations, and sporting events provide students with ways to interact with other age groups and interest groups as well as promote the school atmosphere by addressing individual needs of students in social, academic, and behavioral realms.

Clubs and other organizations are advertised through a handbook/directory or booklet, usually at the beginning of the year. Partnerships have been formed by many schools with businesses to defray the cost of various programs along with providing support to the school.

FOLLOW-UP ACTIVITIES

1. As principal of an at-risk elementary school, you would like to offer some programs or activities that you feel would benefit your population. How would you decide which activities to implement? How would you involve your teachers, P.T.A., or community?

2. Your dean or assistant principal comes to you with a request from the Student Council to establish some incentive programs, such as a breakfast with the principal, awards for outstanding senior, junior, etc. How would you respond to Student Council members?

3. Your school district is interested in starting after-school programs involving technology for students. What steps do you think the school district (or school) should follow to implement a program that would benefit all students?

RESOURCES

Great Ideas for Student Council
NAESP Catalog
1615 Duke Street
Alexandria, Virginia 22314-3483
1-800-386-2377

Las Vegas Parks and Recreation, SAFEKEY
749 Veterans Memorial Dr.
Las Vegas, Nevada 89010
(702) 733-0794

National Association of Elementary School Principals
1615 Duke Street
Alexandria, Virginia 22314
1-800-386-2377

The Path to a Student Council
NAESP Catalog
1615 Duke Street
Alexandria, Virginia 22314-33483
1-800-386-2377

Silverado High School
1650 Silverado High School
Las Vegas, Nevada 891123
(702) 799-5790

6

STUDENT GUIDANCE: PARENTS IN PARTNERSHIP WITH SCHOOLS

Parent involvement in schools plays a significant role in addressing the academic and behavioral needs of students. Educators have long recognized how important it is to engage parents in the educational process, but once again societal changes regarding working parents have had an impact on the availability of parents to be actively involved in the school. Successful schools find ways to develop strong home–school relationships. Anne Henderson cites seven key facts related to parent involvement.

1. The family provides the child's first educational environment.
2. Involving parents in their children's formal education boosts student achievement.
3. Parent involvement is most effective when it is thorough, long-lasting, and well planned.
4. The benefits are not limited to early childhood or the elementary level; there are strong effects from involving parents clear through high school.

5. Involving parents in their own children's educational home is not enough. To ensure that schools serve the community well, parents must be involved at all levels in the school.
6. Children from low-income and minority families have the most to gain when schools involve parents. Parents do not have to be well educated to help.
7. We cannot look at the school and the home apart from one another; we must see how they work with each other and with the world at large.

While school partnerships usually include not only parents but also the community at large, this chapter will focus primarily on the different ways that parents can participate in the educational process, both at home and at the school. Specific programs will be reviewed related to:

- involving parents in planning and shared decision making
- effective communication with parents
- creating parent networks
- involving parents as instructional partners

Parental involvement in schools translates to better communication between the home and the school. According to effective schools research (Lezotte, 1991), parents' understanding and support of the school's basic mission play an important role in helping the school to achieve their goals. According to Lezotte, over the last few years, the role of parents has moved from an emphasis on parents as political allies to parents as true partners. Parents should be made to feel they have an important role in achieving the school's mission. Schools with a strong commitment to home-school relations ensure the following:

- a structure for involving parents in decision making related to school programming
- consistent communication about the mission and goals of the school

- numerous opportunities for parent involvement and support of programs
- the development of ongoing parent education program and materials
- consistent communication about student progress and achievement

PARENT INVOLVEMENT IN PLANNING

The Parent Teacher Association (PTA) is perhaps the most familiar of all parent organizations that takes an active role in supporting the needs of the children nationally, at a state level, and within the local school. The role of the PTA is to address issues that concern children, keep parents advised of current issues, be a political advocate for children, and support local schools by being actively involved.

Most schools have some type of organized parent group even if it is not affiliated with the National PTA. Parent Teacher Organizations (PTO) are formed at some schools with similar goals as the PTA but with less formal structure; they primarily impact the local school with which they are affiliated. Parent Advisory Committees are often used by secondary schools as a means of gaining input, communicating about the instructional program, and involving parents in decision making related to school issues. Over the last few years there has been an increased emphasis on parents taking an active role in school programming, well beyond roles of the past, which primarily involved parents in fund-raising efforts, booster activities, and as sponsors of school events and field trips.

Shared decision making involving parents and the community, sometimes referred to as site-based decision making, has become law in many states. For example, the Texas Education Code (TEC) requires that ". . . the principal of each school campus, with the assistance of parents, community residents, and the professional staff of the school as provided through the procedure established in Section 21.930 of this code, shall establish academic and other performance objectives of the campus . . . " (section 21.7532). The expectation of such laws is that there be broad involvement of school stakeholders in determining the future development of schools.

As a part of site-based decision making, many schools have implemented school site planning teams that include parents and other community members. There is no blueprint for involving parents in curriculum and instructional planning; the avenue and level of the involvement must be tailored to the unique makeup of each school community. Many educators have been hesitant to involve parents in curriculum and instructional decisions; however, schools that have approached parents as advocates rather than adversaries have found that the home-school partnership can significantly contribute to the success of students.

Successful implementation of shared decision making that involves parents and other school stakeholders requires careful planning and thought. An understanding of how the roles and relationships of those involved change as new players are added to the decision-making process is critical. As a school administrator it is important to recognize that the traditional ways of conducting the everyday business of the school may be dramatically challenged through this process. The site administrator must assume the responsibility of orchestrating and managing the shared decision-making process. Such a process requires those involved to engage in collaboration and meaningful dialogue related to common issues rather than competitive argument surrounding special interest issues.

While the task for the site administrator is not an easy one, successful implementation of parental involvement in shared decision making gives responsible parents a chance to participate in charting the course of the schools their children attend and often creates allies as opposed to critics. Keeping in mind the primary goal, which is to increase student achievement by strengthening the overall academic program, will assist the administrator in being persistent when conflicts and frustrations occur—and be assured they will occur.

COMMUNICATION WITH PARENTS

Schools, either public or private, have the responsibility of keeping parents informed regarding the school program. Communication with parents is usually done at two levels, the first relates to schoolwide issues such as curriculum implementation, the identification and implementation of improvement goals, the announcement of scheduled activities and other programming that impacts the entire school. The second level comes directly from the classroom teacher to the parent regarding student progress and achievement.

SCHOOLWIDE COMMUNICATION

Schools should take every opportunity to acquaint parents with school programs, particularly those that directly impact students. Many parents become critical of curriculum programs and teaching methods because they do not fully understand why particular programs have been implemented. Educators often spend a great deal of time researching, studying, and implementing new methods and strategies in an attempt to better address the needs of students and often spend little effort in making parents aware of the changes and involving them in the decision. At the earliest level, parents should be involved in the research, study, and implementation of innovations or program changes.

The most common means of communicating with parents concerning schoolwide programs is through the school newsletter published by the school administrator or through the parent organization. This is certainly an appropriate way of keeping parents informed; however, it is probably not adequate if it is the only communication tool. Katz-McMillan Cooperating Schools, Las Vegas, Nevada, created curriculum brochures that were distributed to all parents at the beginning of the year in an attempt to make them aware of how language arts and mathematics were being taught at the school. The brochures were reader friendly and briefly explained the rationale and philosophy behind the instructional programs. Look-fors were identified so that parents knew what should be happening in each classroom related to reading, writing, spelling, and mathematics.

Communication regarding schoolwide programs should not be limited to printed materials. Frequent opportunities for parents to dialogue with school personnel regarding school programs should be provided. Some schools have implemented Brown Bag luncheon sessions inviting parents to dialogue about the curriculum and instructional programs at the school. The school's parent organization may sponsor meetings that focus on specific issues related to curriculum. School-sponsored Family Academic Nights, where students and parents come together to do reading, writing, and mathematics activities, have been successful.

Involving students in the communication process is also an effective means of keeping parents and the community informed regarding school programming. Student involvement in creating classroom and school newsletters not only assists in communication efforts but also provides students valuable writing and journalism experience. High school journalism clubs are frequently responsible for designing, writing, and publishing school brochures and other department and schoolwide information documents.

An effective means of communication being used by many schools and school districts is through online Internet computer services. School-created home pages that are on the World Wide Web allow parents to access information about the school from their home. School home pages may be as simple as listings of scheduled activities or may include extensive curriculum information. James I. Gibson Elementary School, Henderson, Nevada, effectively utilizes this technology to communicate with parents, the community, and other schools. For further information contact:

>Dr. Peggy Moore
>James I. Gibson Elementary School
>271 Leisure Circle
>Henderson, Nevada 89104
>(702) 799-8730
>http://members.aol.com/glenacem/index.htm

COMMUNICATION ABOUT STUDENT PROGRESS

Parents must be kept well informed regarding student progress and achievement if there is to be a meaningful home-school partnership. Communication regarding student progress usually includes such things as parent-teacher conferences, informal progress reports sent periodically throughout a grading period, and the formal report card, which is summative in nature.

The parent-teacher conference is a valuable means of interacting with parents and establishing a good working relationship. However, effective parent-teacher conferences do not just happen; they require careful planning. The teacher should assume the lead in setting the tone for the conference and be well prepared in order to ensure a successful conference. The following suggestions might be helpful in planning for a parent-teacher conference:

- ♦ The teacher's greeting should be friendly and relaxed. If the teacher is hurried or tense, the parent will know it.
- ♦ Begin with a positive statement of the student's abilities. This conveys interest and liking for the student.
- ♦ The teacher should listen and then listen some more. The parent-teacher conference is not a time for the teacher to deliver a lecture but rather to enlist the support of the parent in meeting the needs of the child. It is important to find out what the parent is thinking and feeling about his or her child.
- ♦ A feeling of cooperation is more easily established if the teacher is not seated behind a desk for the conference. Behind the desk, the teacher is in the position of authority, not partnership.
- ♦ Teachers should be prepared to discuss the child's academic and/or behavioral progress and should be prepared to show samples of student work.
- ♦ It is never productive to argue with parents. Arguing will arouse resentment and resistance.
- ♦ Avoid using blanket words such as *immaturity* and *insecurity*. These are subjective judgments and often create resistance; they may be misinterpreted as a form of criticism.

- Teachers should close the conference on a constructive, pleasant, and positive note. Making plans for further consultations, setting a definite date for the next conference, and restating a plan for cooperative action indicates to the parent the teacher's commitment to addressing the needs of his or her child.

Assisting parents in planning for the conference will increase the probability that the conference will be productive. Providing parents with specific suggestions regarding preparation for the conference, such as questions to ask, things to think about, and a brief description of what will be discussed at the conference sets parents at ease and helps to eliminate the fear of negativism many parents often associate with conferences. At the end of this chapter are sample forms and letters that can be used in assisting parents and teachers in planning for parent-teacher conferences (Documents 6.1–6.3).

Student Progress Reports are used by many teachers as a means of consistently communicating with parents regarding student achievement and behavior. Progress reports usually serve as an interim communication with parents prior to the more formal report card. The frequency with which progress reports are sent out varies from school to school, and often within the school. In the elementary school, primary grade teachers often send weekly progress reports, while intermediate grade teachers may elect to send progress reports every two or three weeks. At the secondary level, interim progress reports are usually sent only in cases where student progress is unsatisfactory or the student is failing. Unfortunately such unsatisfactory notices are viewed as a means to document parent notification rather than a meaningful attempt to enlist parents in helping to solve the problem.

Progress reports should reflect behavioral and curriculum expectations at the school and of the teacher. Utilizing terminology consistent with what will be reported on the summative report card helps to acquaint parents with the curriculum and assessment measures used at the school. Documents 6.4–6.7 include samples of interim student progress reports.

Parent Network/Support Groups

Providing parents the opportunity to network with other parents is an effective way of creating communication support groups for parents. Parent network/support groups have been formed by some schools in the areas of ADHD/ADD, substance abuse, special education, and discipline. Such groups are formed because parents have a common concern or need. These types of groups have been effective in providing parents the opportunity to dialogue with others who share their concern and assist in identifying available resources within the community.

Green Valley High School, Henderson, Nevada, took a proactive approach to parents supporting parents by establishing the Best Parent Network. The purpose of the Best Parent Network is to provide a vehicle whereby all parents can unite to enhance parent, youth, school, and community communication in order to develop age-appropriate activities and standards for youth. Parents were given the opportunity to sign an agreement that they would:

- **ENCOURAGE** wholesome activities for children by actively chaperoning and by not allowing alcohol, tobacco, or any other drug to be consumed by minors who are socializing in their home.
- **COMMUNICATE** with the appropriate adults to ensure that events outside of their home will be actively chaperoned and will not include the use of alcohol, tobacco, or other drug by minors.
- **SUPPORT** and use the legal curfew as minimum standards for their children.
- **BE** a positive role model.
- **MAINTAIN** open lines of communication.

A Best Parent Network Directory is published by the school to provide parents with names of students and a list of parents who signed the agreement. This serves as a ready resource for parents who wish to interact with other parents regarding social events and other school programs.

PARENTS AS INSTRUCTIONAL PARTNERS

Effective parent and community volunteer programs are common in many schools across the country and have proven to be quite successful in establishing and maintaining meaningful communication between the home and the school. Some schools have moved from the traditional use of parent volunteers, which include using parents to duplicate instructional materials, assist in supervision of students on the playground and in the lunchroom, and work in classrooms as an instructional aide, to a more defined role in actually planning and implementing support instructional programs.

ART DOCENT PROGRAM

Many schools in the Clark County School District, Las Vegas, Nevada, have implemented an Art Docent Program in an attempt to connect parents and students in a unique fine arts program. The Art Docent Program is modeled after traditional museum art docent programs with parent volunteers sharing information about the lives of selected artists and discussing enlarged reproductions of the artist's work. Students' exposure to this museum experience enables them to better appreciate the role of the artist and arts in society and allows parents to make a significant contribution to the instructional program of the school.

Schools that do not have an art specialist who is available to enlist and work with parents in establishing an Art Docent Program may work to establish a partnership with local museums or art galleries within the community. For more information regarding an Art Docent Program contact:

Irene Palamar, Art Specialist
Martin Luther King Jr. Elementary School
2260 N. Betty Lane
Las Vegas, Nevada 89115
(702) 799-7390

STUDENT PUBLISHING CENTER

A program that has received national recognition from Secretary of Education Richard W. Riley as an exemplary case of parent involvement is the P.A.W. Student Publishing Center at Katz-McMillan Cooperating Schools, Las Vegas, Nevada. The P.A.W. Center (Publishing Authors' Writings) was developed by the reading improvement teacher, Mrs. Ann Entzel, for the purpose of involving students in the writing process, from early writing drafts to published manuscripts.

When the publishing center was initiated, Mrs. Entzel enlisted parent volunteers to work in the center assisting students with the publication of their work. Materials were developed to assist parents in their work with students, and training was provided in the use of word processors and computers. From the beginning of the project parent volunteers became an integral part of the publishing center; after the first year parents assumed full responsibility for running the publishing center.

Initial student writing begins in the classroom directed by the classroom teachers. When the student writing is ready for publication, students are scheduled into the publishing center. It is at this level that parents take over and guide students through the step-by-step publication process. The P.A.W. Student Publishing Center is solely operated by parent volunteers in close cooperation with the school staff and administration. Parent coordinators handle scheduling, training, and basic center maintenance. A staff coordinator monitors the program and provides workshops to teachers in the writing process to enhance the benefits of the program and to ensure that teachers understand that the purpose of the center is to provide the students the opportunity for self-expression, not for the production of class assignments.

Mrs. Molly Millman, parent coordinator, has been involved with the publishing center since the first year it was established and is responsible for the development of parent training materials. Mrs. Millman has been enlisted by many schools as a consultant in organizing and establishing a parent-coordinated student publishing center. For further information related to this parent volunteer program contact:

Molly Millman
7112 Carrondale
Las Vegas, NV 89128
(702) 363-9936

Enlisting Parent Volunteers

Parent volunteers are usually enlisted at the beginning of the school year. Document 6.8 at the end of this chapter is a Volunteer Sign-up Form used at the elementary school level. It provides parents the opportunity to indicate an interest in volunteering to assist in the classroom, with schoolwide programs, or with special school events. It is suggested the sign-up form be run on three different pages, each a different color, so that when the form is returned the various sections can be distributed to persons responsible for organizing the different activities and programs. Once parents have been enlisted it is important to provide some education and guidance so that the volunteer experience is meaningful for both the parents and the school. Documents 6.9 and 6.10 may be used in an orientation with parents or included in a volunteer handbook. Parent volunteers at the secondary level are most frequently enlisted by specific departments, organizations, or clubs as sponsors or boosters.

In a recent publication of the Office of Education Research and Improvement, U.S. Department of Education, entitled *Reaching All Families* (1996), the idea of Parent Liaisons was identified as a possible means of providing continuity for the school's parent involvement initiatives. Parent liaisons might serve as volunteers or be hired on a part-time basis to assist the school in coordinating parent education events, assisting with outreach to traditionally nonparticipating families, and organizing orientation sessions for new families.

Enlisting and educating parents to work in the school setting is important, but it is also important that school volunteers be recognized for their efforts. Taking the time to say thanks with a personal note, acknowledgment in the school newsletter, a luncheon or tea recognizing parent volunteers, or a small gift at the end of the school year are different ways to let parents know that their efforts are appreciated. Acknowledging parent volunteers need not be expensive or elaborate to be effective. Document 6.11 is a sample of a parent recognition effort.

Summary

Schools have an ever-increasing challenge to provide for the academic, social, and behavioral needs of students. By eliciting parent volunteers and parent support groups, a message of working together to create a home–school partnership is communicated. When parents feel that they are a part of the school's decision-making process and have input in their child's education, everyone benefits.

There is a feeling that the school belongs to all: administrators, support staff, teachers, students, and parents.

Follow-Up Activities

1. Collect samples of school newsletters from five or six schools, including elementary, middle school, and high school. Review the newsletters in terms of identified parent involvement opportunities. Were there any noted differences between elementary and secondary schools regarding the request for or acknowledgment of parent involvement?

2. Identify a school that has an active Parent Advisory Committee or has a School Site Planning Team that includes parents and interview the administrator in terms of the parents' role on the committee. If possible, attend one of the meetings or interview a parent who is involved on the committee. Based on your interactions and observations, do you feel this is a meaningful way to involve parents in the school program?

3. A new teacher at the school has scheduled a conference with the parents of a student to discuss some serious academic and behavioral concerns. The teacher comes to you, as the administrator, asking for assistance in preparing for the conference. He/She has been told by other teachers that these parents will be defensive and uncooperative. What are some things you can do as the administrator to as-

sist this teacher in preparing for the conference? What are some things you might do to increase the chances of this being a positive experience for both the teacher and the parents?

RESOURCES

Effective Schools
Lawrence W. Lezotte, Ph. D.
2199 Jolly Road, Suite 160
Okemos, Michigan 48864
(517) 349-8841
FAX (517) 349-8852

National Association of Partners in Education
901 N. 5th Street
Alexandria, Virginia 22314
(703) 836-4880

Parent Communication
Dr. Peggy Moore
James I. Gibson Elementary School
271 Leisure Circle
Henderson, Nevada 89014
(702) 799-8730

Parent Institute
P.O. Box 7474
Fairfax Station, Virginia
(703) 323-9170

Reading All Families-Creating Family-Friendly Schools
U.S. Department of Education
Partnership for Family Involvement in Education
600 Independence Av., SW
Washington, DC 20202-8173
FAX (210) 401-3036

Texas Business and Education Coalition
400 West 15th St., Suite 910
Austin, Texas 78701
(512) 480-8232

Volunteers - Art Docent
Irene Palamar, Art Specialist
Martin Lurther King Jr. Elementary School
2260 N. Betty Lane
Las Vegas, Nevada 89115
(702) 799-7390

Volunteers - Publishing Center
Molly Millman
7112 Carrondale
Las Vegas, Nevada 89128
(702) 363-9936

Document 6.1 Confirmation of a Parent-Teacher Conference

Dear Parents,

    A parent-teacher conference is one of the many steps we are taking to work with you to build your child's educational program. We will discuss your child's progress in school and learn more about him or her from you.

A PARENT-TEACHER CONFERENCE GIVES YOU A CHANCE TO:
- get to know your child's teacher or teachers
- learn about the school and curriculum
- discuss your child's strengths and weaknesses in various areas

And WE will learn things from YOU that will help us improve your child's educational program!

HERE'S WHAT YOU CAN DO TO GET READY FOR THE CONFERENCE:
1. Make a list of things that will help the teacher understand your child better. For example:
   - any special health needs or learning problems
   - outside interests and hobbies
   - feelings about school
   - reading and study habits
2. Make a list of special things you want to find out from the teacher. For example, you may wish to know about:
   - special services and programs
   - discipline
   - homework
   - health and safety programs
   - opportunities for parent involvement

THE TEACHER MAY DISCUSS WITH YOU:
- your child's test results and what they mean
- what subjects your child is taking and how he/she is doing
- your child's strengths and weaknesses in school
- any observations that can be helpful -- whether the child may have trouble hearing or seeing, etc.

And . . . .
The teacher may have some suggestions or ideas you can use at home to help your child in school.

Conference Schedule: Date _____ Time _____ Place _____

Child's Name _____

DOCUMENT 6.2 PLANNING FOR A PARENT-TEACHER CONFERENCE

Dear Parent:

You and I are going to talk about someone very special next week. That someone special, of course, is your child.

When we meet at parent-teacher conferences next week, I'll be talking about these things:
* how your child is doing
* what we've done and plan to do in our class
* how you and I can work together as partners to provide the best possible education for your child

You probably have some things you'd like to talk about too, things like homework, how you can help at home and, perhaps, school policies. It helps if you write down the things you want to discuss before you come to the conference. That's why I've left some space below. Write down questions and comments you have. Then, bring this note with you to our meeting.

QUESTIONS YOU HAVE ABOUT YOUR CHILD

_____
_____
_____
_____

After our conference, there may be some things we can do to better meet the needs of your child. We'll write those things in the space below during our meeting.

I LOOK FORWARD TO SEEING YOU ON _____
AT _____

Child's Name _____

THANKS FOR HELPING ME HELP YOUR CHILD!

                                                Teacher's Signature

Document 6.3 Planning for a Parent-Teacher Conference

> OUR CONFERENCE IS COMING UP SOON

Dear Parent:

Our teacher-parent conference is schedule for _____.
                                                        Date

It will help our communication during the conference if you take the time to answer a few questions about _____ before we meet.
             Child's Name

Please bring this form with you.

Sincerely,

_____
         Teacher's Signature

* * * * *

What subjects does your child enjoy? _____

How does your child feel about school? _____

Does your child understand the classroom rules? _____

How do you feel about your child's experience in school? _____

_____

_____

Does your child seem to understand how to do homework assignments? _____

_____

Please jot down any topics you would like to discuss with me. _____

_____

_____

_____

Document 6.4 Parent Contact

Name of Student:_____

       Date_____

I am sorry to report that in spite of repeated discussions and counseling, _____ is doing unsatisfactory or failing work in the following area(s):_____

_____

This unsatisfactory progress is the result of:

- Not working in class
- Not handing in homework
- Not completing make-up assignments
- Hurrying through daily work
- Consistently scoring poorly on tests and quizzes
- Excessive absences
- Other:_____

ADDITIONAL INFORMATION:_____

_____

_____

There is sufficient time before the end of the grading period for your child to improve in these areas. If you have any questions, please call the school and leave a message. I will return your call as soon as possible. Thank you.

                                                                _____

                                                                     Signature of Teacher

Please sign the attached copy and have your child return it to school.

_____

Signature of Parent

DOCUMENT 6.5 PROGRESS REPORT

NAME: _____

FOR THE WEEK OF: _____

SUBJECT AREA	3 - EXCEEDS STANDARDS	2 - MEETS STANDARDS	1 - LIMITED PROGRESS
READING			
WRITING			
MATH			
FOLLOWING DIRECTIONS			
RESPECT FOR OTHERS			
ASSIGNMENTS COMPLETE			

TEACHER COMMENTS, IF ANY: _____

_____

PARENT COMMENTS, IF ANY: _____

_____

DEAR PARENTS,

WERE YOU ABLE TO REVIEW YOUR CHILD'S WORK FOR THE WEEK? ___YES ___NO
PLEASE SIGN THIS FORM AND HAVE YOUR CHILD RETURN IT ON MONDAY.

PARENT/GUARDIAN SIGNATURE _____ **DATE** _____

THANK YOU VERY MUCH FOR YOUR SUPPORT! _____
                                                    SIGNATURE OF TEACHER

155

DOCUMENT 6.6 PROGRESS REPORT

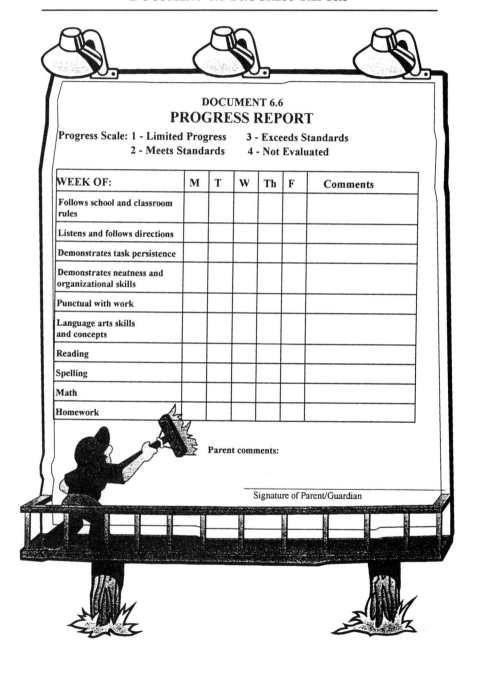

DOCUMENT 6.6
PROGRESS REPORT

Progress Scale: 1 - Limited Progress   3 - Exceeds Standards
                 2 - Meets Standards   4 - Not Evaluated

WEEK OF:	M	T	W	Th	F	Comments
Follows school and classroom rules						
Listens and follows directions						
Demonstrates task persistence						
Demonstrates neatness and organizational skills						
Punctual with work						
Language arts skills and concepts						
Reading						
Spelling						
Math						
Homework						

Parent comments:

Signature of Parent/Guardian

DOCUMENT 6.7 PROGRESS REPORT

STUDENT PROGRESS REPORT
GRADING PERIOD: _____

STUDENT:_____ DATE:_____
TEACHER:_____ GRADE LEVEL:_____

Dear Parents,

This report is to indicate the student's current grade in each subject area.

SUBJECT	GRADES EARNED TO THIS DATE	ADDITIONAL COMMENTS
Language Arts		
Mathematics		
Reading		
Social Studies		
Science		

Student needs to work on the areas indicated below:
___ Listening
___ Following directions
___ Completing homework
___ Talking at appropriate times
___ Using time wisely
___ Playground behavior
___ Working independently
___ Neatness in work
___ Class cooperation

Parents, please review this report, sign it, and return it to school. If there are any concerns or questions please do not hesitate to call me at school.

_____   _____
Signature of Student   Signature of Parent/Guardian

Comments:_____
_____
_____

DOCUMENT 6.8 VOLUNTEER SIGN-UP FORM

 # VOLUNTEER

Volunteers working in classrooms and in various capacities throughout the school have been a real asset to the instructional program. Once again we want to give you the opportunity to be involved in your child's educational process by participating in some facet of our school. Because we know it is not possible for all parents to come in on a regular basis, we have defined three different areas where volunteers are needed. These include classroom activities, schoolwide programs, and special events. Grandparents are also encouraged to participate. Please fill out the demographic information on each page where you indicate an interest so that we can easily distribute the information to those responsible for enlisting and coordinating our volunteer efforts.

SECTION I - CLASSROOM

Please indicate your interest and prioritize your preference if you mark more than one (i.e., #1, #2, #3, etc.).

_____ Make educational games to be used in the classroom

_____ Read or record a story for children

_____ Listen to children read

_____ Tutor children in math or reading

_____ Assist with preparing daily instructional materials

_____ Work with children in writing books

_____ Help with setting up classroom parties

_____ Sharing travel adventures

Other _____

Volunteer's Name _____ Phone _____

Child's Name _____ Grade _____

Teacher's Name _____

Available Times: Monday _____ Time _____ to _____
Tuesday _____ Time _____ to _____
Wednesday _____ Time _____ to _____
Thursday _____ Time _____ to _____
Friday _____ Time _____ to _____

THANKS! THANKS! THANKS! THANKS!

Document 6.8 Volunteer, continued

SECTION II - SCHOOLWIDE PROGRAMS

Please indicate your interest and prioritize your preference if you mark more than one (i.e., #1, #2, #3, etc.).

_____ Student Publishing Center

_____ Assist music teacher in classroom or with other activities

_____ Assist art teacher in classroom or help to mount student work

_____ Assist P.E. teacher in classroom or in other activities

_____ Assist in the lunchroom and on the playground at noon

_____ Piano accompanist for Honors Choir and other musical program

_____ Art Docent Program -- learning about a famous artist and sharing the information with groups of children

_____ Assist with clerical duties in the school office or nurse's office

_____ Work in the student snack store during lunch recess

Volunteer's Name _____ Phone _____

Child's Name _____ Grade _____

Teacher's Name _____

Someone will contact you to share more information about the program you indicated and to determine when you are available to help.

THANKS! THANKS! THANKS! THANKS!

PARENTS IN PARTNERSHIP WITH SCHOOLS

DOCUMENT 6.8 VOLUNTEER, CONTINUED

SECTION III - SPECIAL EVENTS

Please indicate your interest and prioritize your preference if you mark more than one (i.e., #1, #2, #3, etc.).

_____ PTA Activities

_____ Fall Carnival

_____ Spring Family Night

_____ School Pictures

_____ Our family owns a business and would like to be involved in a business partnership with the school. The business is _____.

Volunteer's Name _____   Phone_____

Child's Name _____   Grade _____

Teacher's Name _____

Someone will contact you to share more information about the program you indicated and to determine when you are available to help.

THANKS! THANKS! THANKS! THANKS!

Document 6.9 Effective Ways to Work with Children

1. Be warm and friendly. Learn the children's names and show interest in what they are doing and telling you. You are very important as a listener.

2. When working with children, encourage them to do their own thinking. Give them plenty of time to answer; silence often means they are thinking and organizing what they want to say or write.

3. If you don't know an answer or are unsure of what to do, admit it to the children and work it out together. Feel free to ask the teacher or children for help when you need it.

4. Use tact and positive comments to encourage children. Seek something worthy of a compliment, especially when children are having difficulties.

5. Accept each child as she/he is. You do not need to feel responsible for judging a child's abilities, progress, or behavior.

6. If a child is upset, encourage him/her to talk the problem over with you. You need not solve the problem, but by listening and talking you help the child feel you care.

7. Respect a child's privacy. Personal information shared by a child should be regarded as confidential; however, if a child reveals information regarding his/her personal safety, you should speak with the classroom teacher or principal.

8. Maintain a sense of humor.

9. Be consistent with teacher's rules for classroom behavior, schedule, and atmosphere.

10. Wear clothes that are consistent with the school's dress code.

11. If parents and friends ask about your work, tell them you enjoy working with the children and discuss the activities you do rather than specific information about the child, teacher, or school. Confidentiality is important.

12. Keep your commitment; the children will expect you and look forward to your coming. If you know you will be gone, tell them in advance. Keep all promises, and make none that you cannot keep. Children never forget!

Document 6.10 Ways Volunteers Can Help

1. Tell stories to children
2. Listen to children read
3. Conduct flash card drills
4. Provide individual help
5. Assist in learning centers
6. Set up learning centers
7. Reproduce materials
8. Work in the library
9. Practice vocabulary with non-English speaking students
10. Make instructional games
11. Play instructional games
12. Play games at recess
13. Grade papers
14. Work with underachievers
15. Assist with field trips
16. Make props for plays
17. Help children with arts and crafts
18. Help with cooking projects
19. Check out books from the public library
20. Set up experiments
21. Collect lunch money
22. Escort students to lunchroom, library, and bathroom
23. Prepare teaching materials
24. Supervise groups taking tests
25. Talk to children -- be a friend
26. Play musical instrument
27. Help students who play instruments
28. Make puppets
29. Help with handwriting practice
30. Drill spelling words
31. Share ethnic backgrounds and experiences
32. Assist in preparing courses in photography, creative dramatics, knitting, and square dancing
33. Secure materials from the library

Document 6.11 Parent Recognition

7

SELECTED REFERENCES

Beck, R., & Gabriel, S. *(1988). Project R.I.D.E. program manual* (3rd ed.). Great Falls, MT: Great Falls Public Schools.

Bedley, G. (1980). *How do you recognize a good school when you walk into one?* Irvine, CA: People-Wise.

Bedley, G. (1992). *The big R responsibility.* Irvine, CA: People-Wise.

Blanck, G. (1990). *Vygotsky and education: Instructional implications and applications of sociohistorical psychology.* New York: Cambridge University Press.

Cahoon, P. (1987/88). Mediator magic. *Educational Leadership, 45,* 92-94.

Clewell, B., & Joy, M. (1993). Choice in Montclair, New Jersey: A policy information paper. In D. Walrip, W. Marks, & N. Estes (Eds.), *Magnet school policy studies and evaluations.* (p. 61). Austin, TX: Morgan Printing.

Curwin, R., & Mendler, A. (1988). *Discipline with dignity.* Alexandria, VA: ASCD.

Erikson, E.H. (1963). *Childhood and society* (2nd ed.). New York: Norton.

Gibbs, J. (1987). *TRIBES: A process for social development and cooperative learning.* Santa Rosa, CA: Center Source Publishers.

Huff, A. L. (1995). Flexible block scheduling: It works for us. *NASSP Bulletin, 79* (571), 95.

Kruse, C. A., & Kruse, G. D. (1995). The master schedule and learning: Improving the quality of education. *NASSP Bulletin, 79* (571), 5.

Labinowicz, E. (1985). *Learning from children.* California: Addison-Wesley.

Lewin, K. (1931). *A handbook of child psychology* (C. Murchism, Ed.). Worcester, MA: Clark University Press.

Musumeci, M., & Szczypkowski, R. (1993). New York State magnet school evaluation study final report. In D. Walrip, W. Marks, & N. Estes (Eds.), *Magnet school policy studies and evaluations* (pp. 95–259). Austin, TX: Morgan Printing.

Piaget, J. (1964). *The moral judgment of the child.* New York: Free Press.

Slavin, R.E. (1994). *Educational psychology theory and practice* (4th ed.). Boston, MA: Allyn and Bacon.

Trudge, J. (1990). *Vygotsky and education: Instructional implications and applications of sociohistorical psychology.* New York: Cambridge University Press.

Vygotsky, L.S. (1978). *Mind in society: The development of higher psychological processes.* (M. Cole, V. John-Steiner, S. Scribner, & E. Souberman, Eds.) Cambridge, MA: Harvard University Press.

Roland Wallace, Jr.